Maths

through

Story and

Rhyme

A Revision Guide for Key Stages 3 and 4

Sunnil Singh and Narishaa Singh

Published by Sunnil Singh

Edited by:
Narishaa Singh

ISBN 978-0-9558920-0-4

Text, design, layout and original illustrations © Sunnil Singh 2008
Some clipart provided by GSP's 120 000 Royalty free Clipart Images CD
All rights reserved.

Copyright © Sunnil Singh 2008

Contents

Introduction.	3
Our system explained.	4
The number rhyme scheme.	5
The alphabet scheme.	7
The four mathematical operators.	9

Section One - Number

Order of operations	10
Arranging numbers in order.	10
Big numbers.	11
Cross multiply and divide technique.	12
Converting between different units.	13
Factors.	14
Fractions.	15
Imperial and metric units.	18
Number line	22
Negative numbers.	24
Ordering decimals.	25
Percentages.	27
Prime numbers.	29
Ratio.	31
Rounding off.	34
Estimating.	39
Time.	40
Some tricks with multiplication and division.	
o Chinese multiplication	42
o Patterns in 9 times table	43
o Patterns in 11 times table	44
o Patterns in 12 times table	45
o Division by 3 and 9	45
o Division by 11	46
o Multiplying and Dividing by 10, 100, 1000 etc.	47
Recap and review of number.	49

Section Three - Algebra

Number patterns.	81
Number patterns, finding the nth term.	83
Special number sequences.	85
Square roots.	87
Collecting like terms.	88
Balancing: An introduction to equations.	89
Multiplying out brackets.	89
Making formulas using words.	90
Powers.	91
Degrees Celsius and degrees Fahrenheit.	92
Trial and improvement.	93
Recap and review of algebra.	94

Section Two - Shapes

Angles.	50
Angles and parallel lines.	54
Angles in shapes and some others.	57
Shapes.	58
Solids and nets.	60
Regular polygons.	61
Regular polygons interior and exterior angles.	62
Area.	63
Typical questions on area.	66
Perimeter.	67
Volume or capacity.	68
Transformations.	69
Symmetry.	71
Enlargements.	74
Maps.	76
Bearings.	78
Recap and review of shapes.	80

Section Four - Data

Representing data.	95
Tally tables.	99
Graphs.	100
Averages.	103
Frequency tables.	105
Probability.	106
Recap and review of data.	109

Some other bits!

Your revision strategies.	110
Answers: You have a go.	112
Answers: Recap and Review	113

Copyright © Sunnil Singh 2008

Introduction

To excel at any subject you need to both understand and remember information. Maths relies a lot on understanding, but you certainly would not be able to solve any problem if you could not remember basic facts and rules. In this book I will be introducing you to some incredibly fun ways of remembering information. This information will then help you understand and solve those seemingly nasty problems.

Listed below are some of the ways that can be used to remember information. I have used these on their own and sometimes in combination.

1. **Mnemonics** (memory tools).
2. **Patterns in information**
3. **Tricks** (patterns often lead to tricks that make for easier calculation)
4. **Relevance to everyday life**. If information can be related to things that we already know or if it has some sort of meaning for us, then it is easier to remember!

I will discuss mnemonics in greater detail as they have been used often in this book.

Mnemonics or memory tools are methods for remembering information that is otherwise quite difficult to remember.
Our brain stores information easier if it has colour, sound, smell or other sensations related to it.

You certainly will not forget the horrific scene at an accident or a funny scene in a movie. Unfortunately words on a page are difficult to remember because they are dull and boring. However if we can store information with colourful, funny or ridiculous images, then they will be easier to remember.

Our system explained

One method involves the use of *linking one image to another*. For Example try to remember the following shopping list:
Butter, milk, bread, nails and crab (I used a short list just to demonstrate).
Now *picture* the objects *associated* to one another in some *crazy, funny* way like I have done.

| Picture a huge block of *butter*. | The butter is then *milked*! | *Bread* then flows out of the milk. | *Nails* in the bread. Ouch! | *Crab* hammers a nail in! |

Another way would be to place all these objects into a little *story*.

Butter was walking along a river of *milk*.

As he was walking, he noticed a boat made of *bread*!

He decided to use the *nail* oars to paddle across.

Suddenly a huge *crab* appeared and ate him!

The problem with maths is that numbers and maths words are difficult to picture or visualize. So we use words that *sound or rhyme* like the words we need. For example; term - think of bus terminal or termite. Factor might be factory and so on…
These images can now be used in our stories.

Term = terminal or termite

Factor = factory

Copyright © Sunnil Singh 2008

A more animated system would be the *number rhyme scheme*. Here we use images of objects that rhyme with the numbers!

1   Gun
2   Shoe
3   Tree
4   Door
5   Hive
6   Sticks
7   Heaven
8   Gate
9   Line
10   Hen

Copyright © Sunnil Singh 2008

Lets' use this system to remember the number pie (π) 3.14….
Remember what each number stands for. Now just *link* those images.

To remember Π (3.14…) think of this little battle:

Pie   in a *tree*   pulls out a *gun*   to shoot at *door*

3   1   4

The number Π (3.14…) is used to find the area of a circle : $A = \Pi r^2$ or circumference of a circle $C = \Pi * d$ (where d = r *2). You often need this number and might be asked for it in a non- calculator paper.

There are other ways to use this system as well. We could *peg each image onto a number*:

Example: to remember that an *octagon has 8 sides* or a nonagon has 9 sides use words that sound, even in part, like the names of the shapes: *Octa*gon sounds like *octo*pus so picture an *octopus used as a gate*! So if someone asks you how many sides in an *octa*gon, you think straightaway of an *octo*pus used as a gate and *gate* makes you think of *8*!
Refer to the section on Regular Polygons.

By far the best technique to use is the *Story technique*. This has the advantage that we remember not only the order of numbers/ facts but that if we forget one part of the story the rest of the story will normally *trigger* / jog your memory to help fill in the gaps. It also prevents us from confusing images that might be used more than once in the book since each image will be imbedded in a unique story. All your story needs is a *trigger image*. This is usually the *heading of the work*.
     Trigger image (heading) linked to *sub-headings* forms a *story*.

Example: If the heading is say Trial and Improvement then picture a courtroom and use this as the setting for the story.

Sometimes it might be difficult to find an image for a maths word and so there is yet another technique that we could use, *The Alphabet Technique*.

We associate images representing *letters of the alphabet* to images you create for the things to be remembered. The images for the letters were created *phonetically* so that the sound of the first syllable of the word is the name of the letter.

Copyright © Sunnil Singh 2008

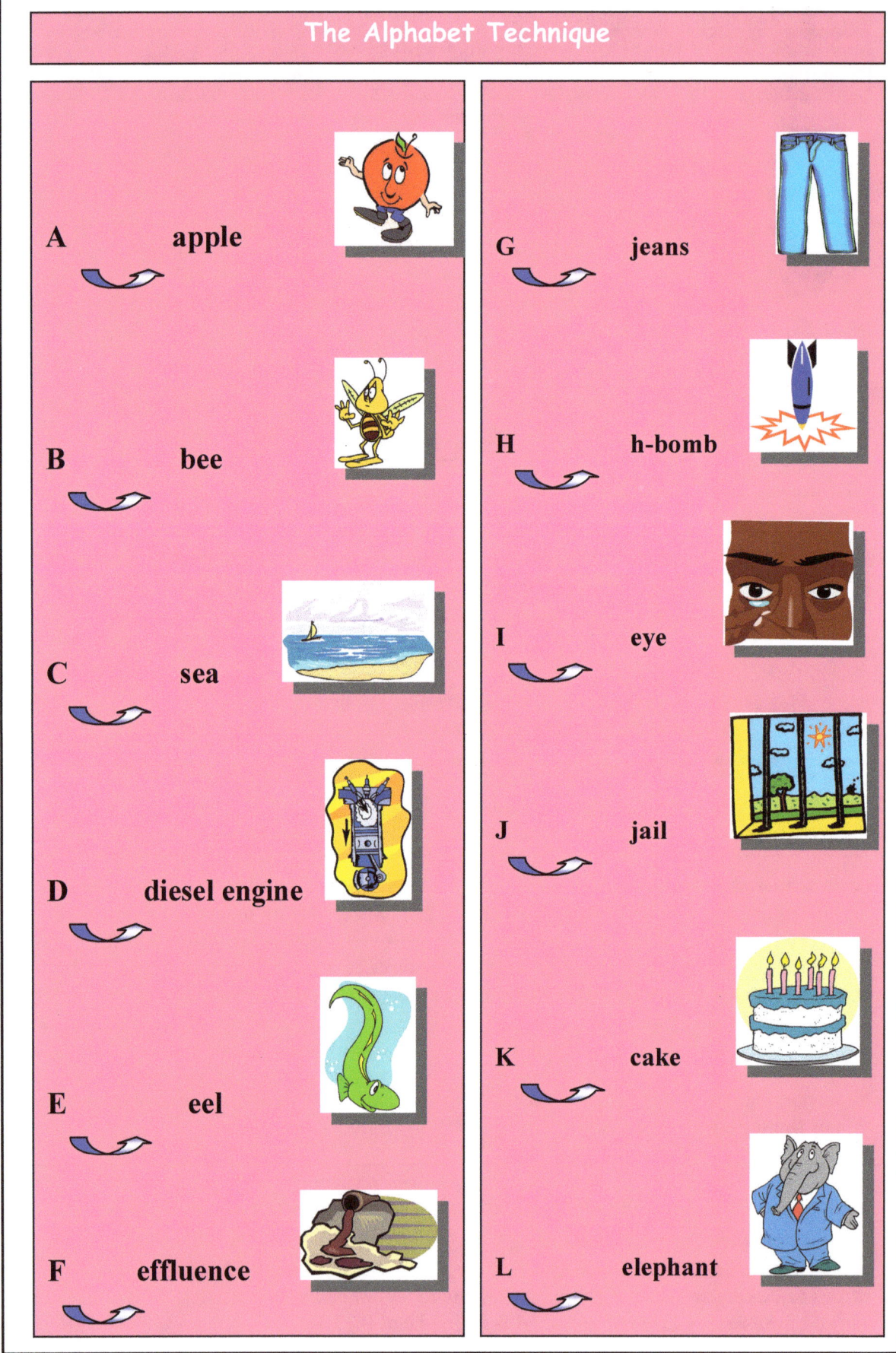

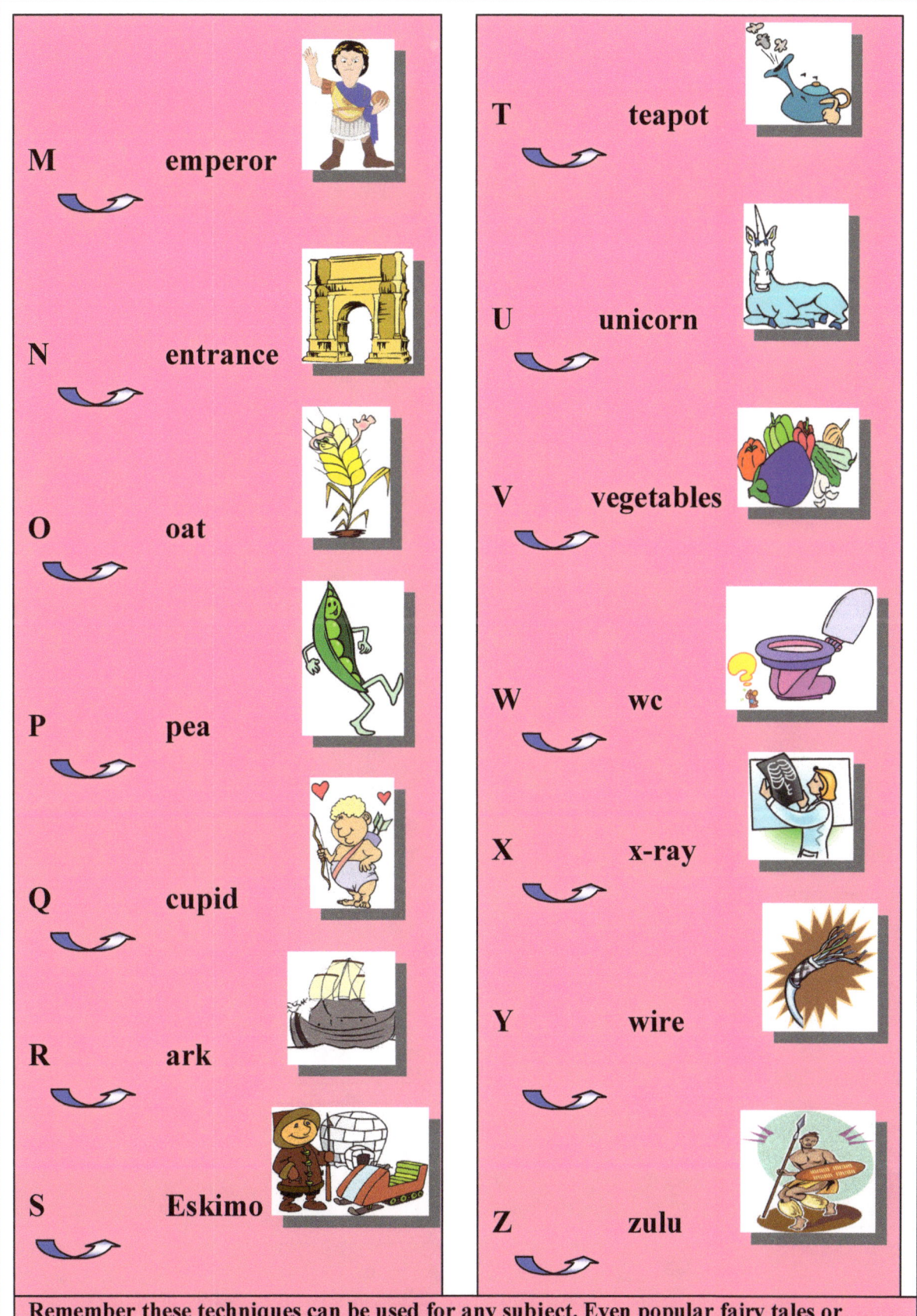

M	emperor	
N	entrance	
O	oat	
P	pea	
Q	cupid	
R	ark	
S	Eskimo	
T	teapot	
U	unicorn	
V	vegetables	
W	wc	
X	x-ray	
Y	wire	
Z	zulu	

Remember these techniques can be used for any subject. Even popular fairy tales or nursery rhymes can be used skilfully. Feel free to use other images that you might prefer, just have fun and be amazed by how much you can learn!

The Four Mathematical Operators.

Meet the characters that will represent our four main operations in maths.

Addition: sounds like: 'a-dish-shine'. We will use a *shiny dish*.

Subtract: sounds like: 'sub –track'. We will use *a submarine on railway tracks*.

Multiply: sounds like 'mule-tea-pie'. We will use a *mule* that is dressed with a *teapot* and some *pie!*

Division: sounds like 'deer-vision'. We will use a *deer* that is *wearing glasses*.

Addition and **Subtraction** are **opposites**.

Multiplication and **Division** are also **opposites**.

12 + 6 = 18   but   18 – 6 = 12
               and   18 – 12 = 6

5 x 6 = 30   but $\frac{30}{5} = 6$ and $\frac{30}{6} = 5$

Just like in **Function machines** you can use the opposite operation to get back to the beginning!

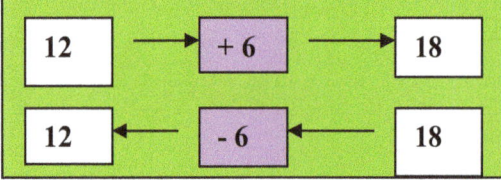

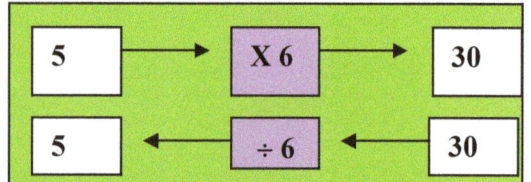

Some other Operators

Greater than, represented by this symbol $>$. Example: $5 > 3$ and $2 > -5$.

Less than, represented by this symbol $<$. Example: $6 < 9$ and $-5 < -1$.

Sometimes we might want to combine the signs.

This symbol $\geq$ means greater than or equal to. This symbol $\leq$ means less than or equal to.

Example: $a > 25$, could be 26, 27….. but $a \geq 25$ would start at 25 (25, 26…).

Copyright © Sunnil Singh 2008

Number

Order of Operations

When a calculation contains a mixture of +,-, x, and ÷, remember the order of operations.

First do	**B**rackets
Then Powers	**O**f
Next do	**D**ivision
And	**M**ultiplication
Then	**A**ddition
And	**S**ubtraction

a) 8 + 6 x 4   BOD**M**A**S**
  = 8 + 24
  = 32

b) 24 − 12 ÷ 6 BO**D**MA**S**
  = 24 −2
  = 22

c) (8 + 4) x 3   **B**OD**M**AS
  = 12 x 3
  = 36

d) 5 x 6^2 − 7   **B**O**D**M**A**S
  = 5 x 36 − 7
  = 180 −7
  = 173

Also called: BIDMAS (**B**rackets, **I**ndices, **D**ivision, **M**ultiplication, **A**ddition and **S**ubtraction)

Arranging numbers in order of size

Picture many numbers, all new recruits at an army base, trying to *line up in order.*

Example: Arrange the following numbers in order of smallest to largest (ascending order).
987   55   144   610   89   233   1597   377

Step one: Arrange in *groups*, with the fewest digits first.

An army officer shouts at them to get into the correct *groups*.

[89   55]   [987   144   610   233   377]   [1597]

Step Two: Now place the numbers within each group *in order.*

Once in their groups, they arrange themselves *in order.*

[55   89]   [144   233   377   610   987]   [1597]

Cool Fact: Number of countries in each of the seven continents from least to most are: Antarctica - (0), South America - (12), Australia - (14), North America - (23), Asia - (44, Europe - (46), Africa - (53).

You have a go: Arrange the following numbers in order:
610   233   55   1597   89   144   377   987

Big numbers

Imagine a *huge number*. He will be the character in our little story.

Large numbers are always read, *in groups of three*, from the right hand side.

Imagine a *huge* number before *three* buildings.

Seems as though he wants to eat them!

Example: 9871597 would be read as:

| 9 | 871 | 597 | ← Start here |

Leave a space after every 3 digits

Read as : nine million eight hundred and seventy one thousand five hundred and ninety seven

Example: 13213455 would be read as:

| 13 | 213 | 455 | ← Start here |

Read as : thirteen million two hundred and thirteen thousand four hundred and fifty five

Cool Fact

Modern man bases time on the second. A day is defined as 86,400 seconds, and a second is officially defined as 9,192,631,770 oscillations of a cesium-133 atom in an atomic clock.

You have a go: Write out the following big number in words: 28657.

Cross multiply and divide technique

This technique will help us especially when we have to convert between different units or more simply to find a new value for a relationship that we already know.

First: arrange the *conversion factor at the top* and then place the question directly below. Remember to keep the *same units on the same side*!

Second: *cross multiply and then divide* your answer by the remaining number.

We will use shapes to represent the numbers since the numbers can change in every question. The position of the number is more important here.

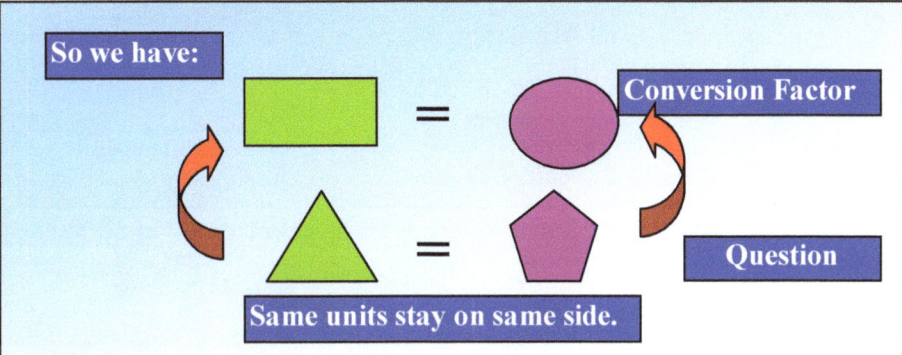

Let's say we wanted to find the value of the *triangle*. We cross multiply and then divide as follows:

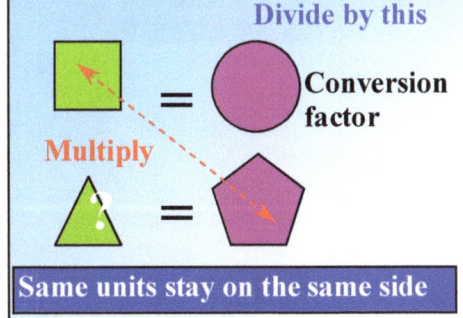

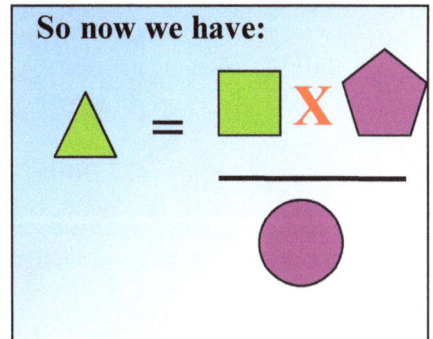

To find the square
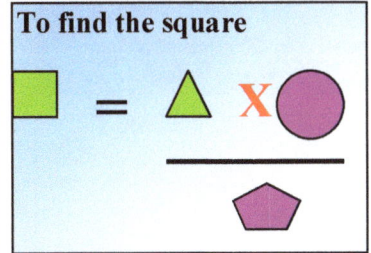

To find the circle
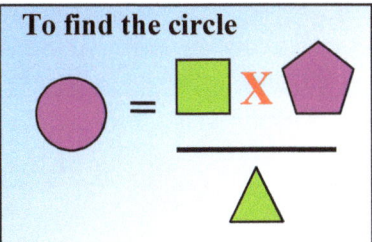

To find the pentagon
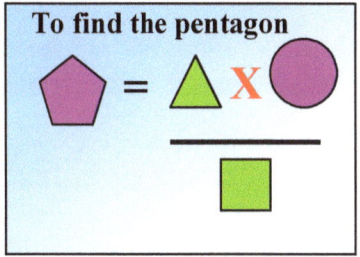

Example: How many centimetres are there in 3 meters?
Solution:

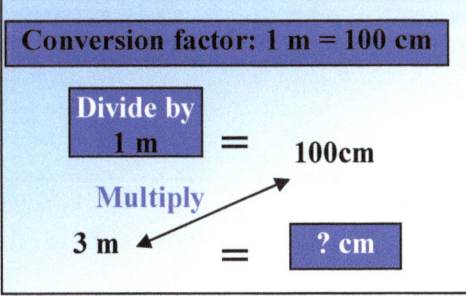

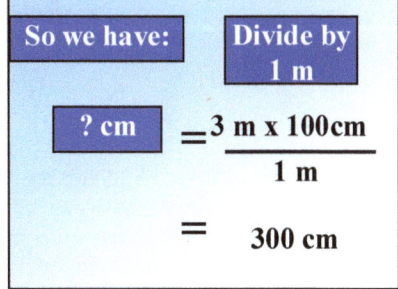

Copyright © Sunnil Singh 2008

Converting between different units

We will use the **cross multiply and divide technique** to convert between different units.

Example: How many minutes in 2 hours?

Conversion factor: 1 hour = 60 minutes

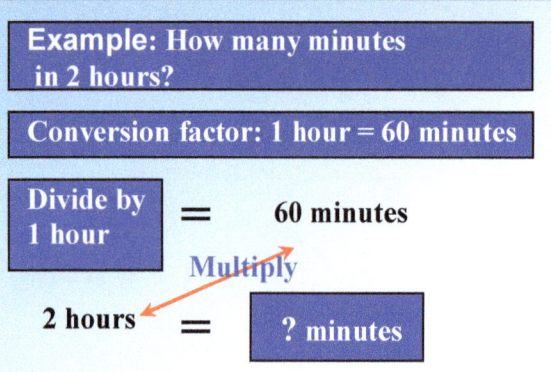

So we have:

? minutes = $\dfrac{2 \times 60}{1}$

= 120 minutes

Example: How many gallons make 56 pints?

Conversion factor: 1 gallon = 8 pints

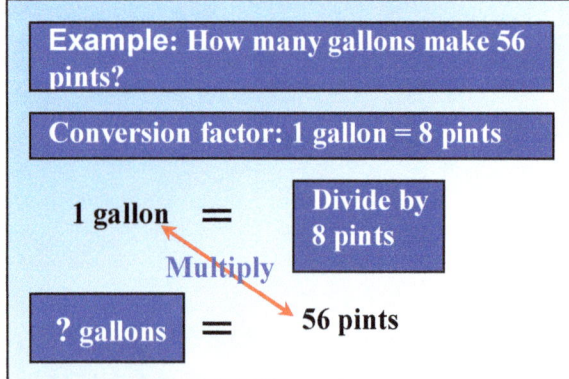

So we have:

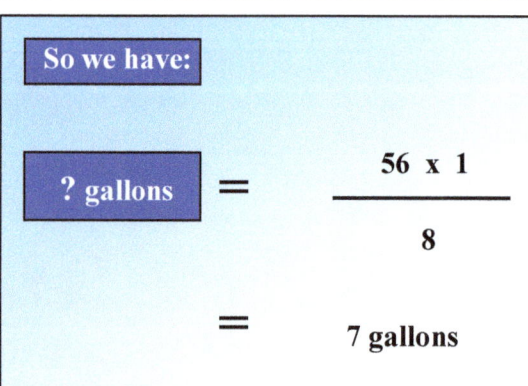

? gallons = $\dfrac{56 \times 1}{8}$

= 7 gallons

Sometimes you might be given the conversion factor. Exchange rates are a good example.

Example: If £ 1 = R 10.20 (South African Rands), then how much is R 15.63 in pounds and pence?

Conversion factor: 1 £ = R 10.20

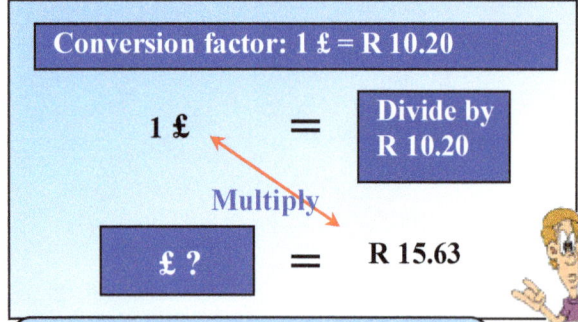

So we have:

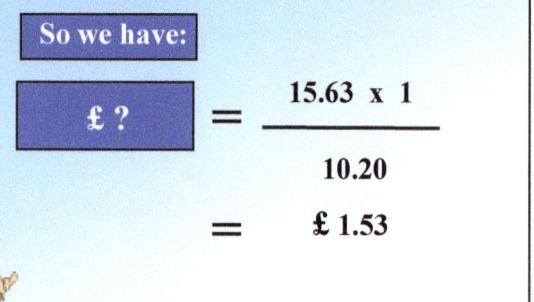

£ ? = $\dfrac{15.63 \times 1}{10.20}$

= £ 1.53

Cool Fact: In 1999 NASA lost the $125 million mars Orbiter because one engineering team used metric units while another used Imperial units for calculation!

You have a go:
If 1 £ = R 13, how many rands will you get for £ 21?

Factors

> Factor sounds like **fact**ory so we will set our story around a factory.

Factors: these are just numbers that *divide exactly into a given number* or you could say *multiply in pairs to give the same number*.

Factors *multiply in pairs* **to give the number.**

Example: 3 x 2 = 6
(3 and 2 are factors of 6)

Factors *divide exactly into* **a given number.**

Example: $^8/_2 = 4$ and $^8/_1 = 8$
(2 and 1 are some of the factors of 8)

Multiplication leads the factors into the factory in *pairs*.

Inside the factory *division* divides up the numbers so that their *factors can fit into them exactly!*

Two ways to find factors:

1. Without a calculator

Example: Find factors of 12.
Find pairs of numbers that multiply to give the number.
 1 x 12 = 12
 2 x 6 = 12
 3 x 4 = 12 (4 x 3 = 12, don't repeat).
 Factors of 12 are: 1, 2, 3, 4, 6 and 12
Once you get to half of the number the only factor left after that is the number itself.

Note: multiplication and division are opposite operations.
 2 x 6 = 12 so 12 ÷ 6 = 2 and 12 ÷ 2 = 6

Cool Fact
Napier's bones is an abacus created by John Napier for calculation of products and quotients of numbers.

2. With a calculator

Example: Find factors of 14.
Using a calculator, just divide 14 repeatedly starting at 1.
Only go up to the halfway mark, which is 7.
14 ÷ 1 = 14
14 ÷ 2 = 7
14 ÷ 3 = 4.6
14 ÷ 4 = 3.5
14 ÷ 5 = 2.8
14 ÷ 6 = 2.3
Not factors since they do not divide exactly!
14 ÷ 7 = 2
Factors of 14 are: 1, 2, 7 and 14

You have a go: **What are factors? Write out the factors of: a) 21 b) 34**

Fractions

"Fraction sounds like **fract**ure so picture our fraction character!"

Fractions are simply *parts of a whole*.

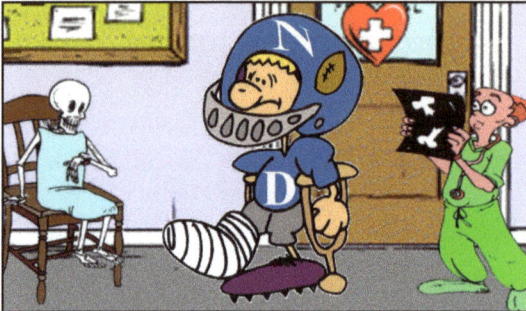

Fraction boy goes to the hospital to be treated.

Some weird doctors break him up into *parts*.

Half of each of these shapes is shaded.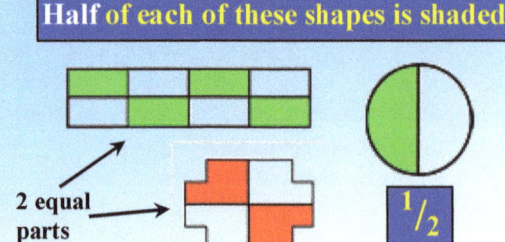

Quarter of each of these shapes is shaded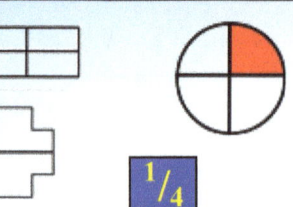

2 equal parts

We can tell what *size the fraction* is by counting the number of *parts that the whole is divided into*.

To put him back together, he is then taken into theatre where a nurse and a doctor try to figure out *what size* he was by *counting the number of parts that he was divided into*.

| ½ | ½ | | ⅓ | ⅓ | ⅓ | | ¼ | ¼ | ¼ | ¼ |

2 parts = half   3 parts = thirds   4 parts = quarters

Every fraction has two parts:

Number at the top — **Numerator**

Number at the bottom — **Denominator**

Copyright © Sunnil Singh 2008

Equivalent Fractions
(Fractions may *look different* but they can have the *same value*).

Fraction emerges from surgery. The surgeons have made a few mistakes. He remembers *how different he used to look*.

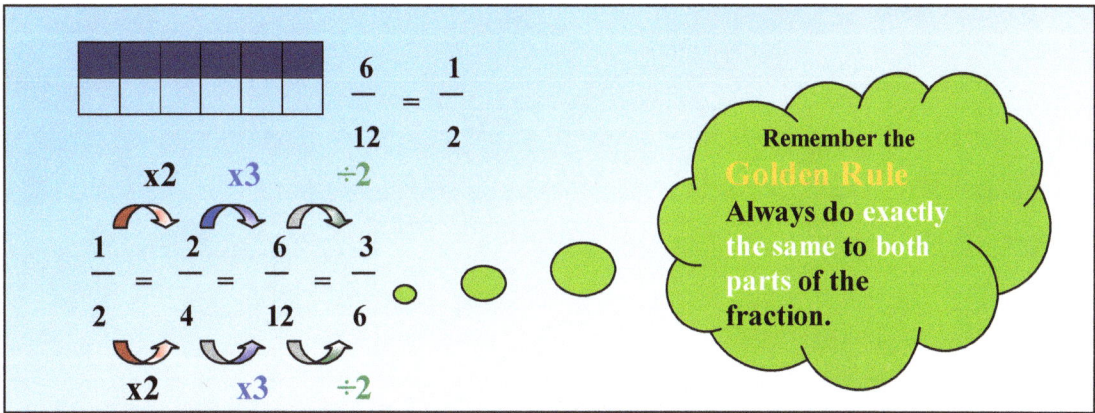

$$\frac{6}{12} = \frac{1}{2}$$

×2 ×3 ÷2

$$\frac{1}{2} = \frac{2}{4} = \frac{6}{12} = \frac{3}{6}$$

×2 ×3 ÷2

Remember the Golden Rule Always do *exactly the same* to *both* parts of the fraction.

Simplifying Fractions

Sounds similar to *simply-frying*. So we picture our fraction character in a frying pan.

As the name suggests we are trying to make to *fraction look simple*. This follows on from equivalent fractions as the simplified fractions *look different but have the same value.*

Find the *largest number* that will *divide* into both the numerator and denominator exactly.

Now that fraction boy has been cooked, *division* decides to eat him and wants to *cut him up* or *divide him up* with the *largest numbers* that he could find!

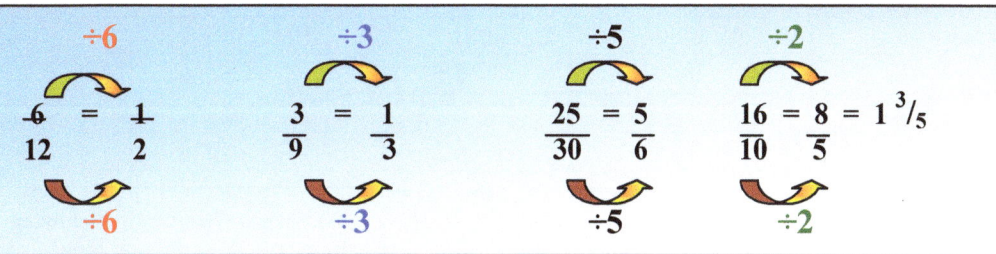

÷6   ÷3   ÷5   ÷2

$$\frac{6}{12} = \frac{1}{2} \quad \frac{3}{9} = \frac{1}{3} \quad \frac{25}{30} = \frac{5}{6} \quad \frac{16}{10} = \frac{8}{5} = 1\,^3/_5$$

÷6   ÷3   ÷5   ÷2

$^8/_5$ is a **Top heavy** or **Improper fraction** (numerator is larger) while $1\,^3/_5$ is a **Mixed number** (has both a whole number and a fraction).

To convert from a Mixed number to an Improper fraction.

Example: Convert $1\frac{3}{5}$ to an improper fraction.

Multiply the denominator and the whole number. Then add this answer to the numerator.

Then add to numerator → 3 (5+3=8)
Multiply (1 x 5) → 5

$\Rightarrow \frac{8}{5}$

Remember: Always keep the same denominator

Examples: $8\frac{1}{3} = \frac{25}{3}$ $7\frac{8}{9} = \frac{71}{9}$

Converting fractions to decimals to percentages.

With a calculator:

Fraction $\frac{3}{5}$ —divide→ Decimal 0.6 —x by 100→ Percentage 60%

Remember: add the percentage sign to your answer!

Without a calculator: Try to make the denominator a multiple of 10, 100 or 1000. Remember to change the numerator in the same way!

x2 : $\frac{3}{5} = \frac{6}{10} = 0.6 = 60\%$ (x100)

x25 : $\frac{3}{4} = \frac{75}{100} = 0.75 = 75\%$ (x100)

Fraction ⇒ Decimal ⇒ Percentage

Make denominator a multiple of 10 or divide on calculator. | x 100

Use this flow chart to help you.

We need to be able to convert between each of them. Look at the following:

Diagram	Fraction	Decimal	Percentage
	$\frac{1}{2}$	0.5	50%
	$\frac{1}{4}$	0.25	25%
	$\frac{1}{5}$	0.2	20%

Cool Fact
At present $1\frac{1}{2}$ acres of rainforest are lost every second with tragic consequences for both developing and industrial countries.

You have a go: Convert the following fractions into decimals and then percentages.
a) $\frac{1}{2}$ b) $\frac{1}{4}$ c) $\frac{1}{3}$ d) $\frac{3}{4}$

Imperial and metric units

Each of these is used as a *conversion factor* for when we have to convert between different units or when we need to find missing values.

Here are a few Metric Units:

Length → mm, cm, m, km
Area → mm², cm², m², km²
Volume → mm³, cm³, m³, litres, ml
Weight → g, kg, tonnes
Speed → km/h, m/s

The conversion factors for these are:
1 cm = 10 mm
1 m = 100 cm
1 km = 1000 m
1 litre = 1000 ml
1 litre = 1000 cm³
1 cm³ = 1 ml
1 tonne = 1000 kg
1 kg = 1000 g

In order to remember these associations we will use the following images. These will be objects normally associated with these units in everyday life or even objects that sound similar to these units.

cm = centipede
Km = long road
Litre = bottle of milk
Tonne = truck
gram = gran
ml = can of pop
kg = bag of rice
1 cm³ = syringe
Metre = metre ruler
mm = millipede

Remember: 10 = hen from our number rhyme scheme.

Copyright © Sunnil Singh 2008

We will also need characters fo the numbers 100 and 1000. Remember from our **number rhyme scheme**: one = gun, two = shoe …ten = hen etc.

Hundred sounds similar to **'hunted'** so picture a **hunter**!
One hundred would be a gun dressed as a hunter
Two hundred would be a shoe dressed as a hunter etc.

Thousand sounds like **'toe-sand'**, so picture a **toe made of sand!**
One thousand would be our toe character but now wearing a gun.

Let our stories begin, but remember that even though $1 = gun$ we will not use it everywhere as it will be confusing! So if it is just 1 unit example: 1 cm or 1 km, then only the units character is shown.

1 cm	10 mm	1 cm = 10 mm
Our *centipede* spots trouble!	*Hen* wants to eat a *millipede* sandwich!	Centipede hits hen and saves millipede.

1 m	100 cm	1 m = 100 cm
Metre is doing some shopping.	*One hundred* stands behind with a *centimetre* gun.	Quick cash! He holds up metre.

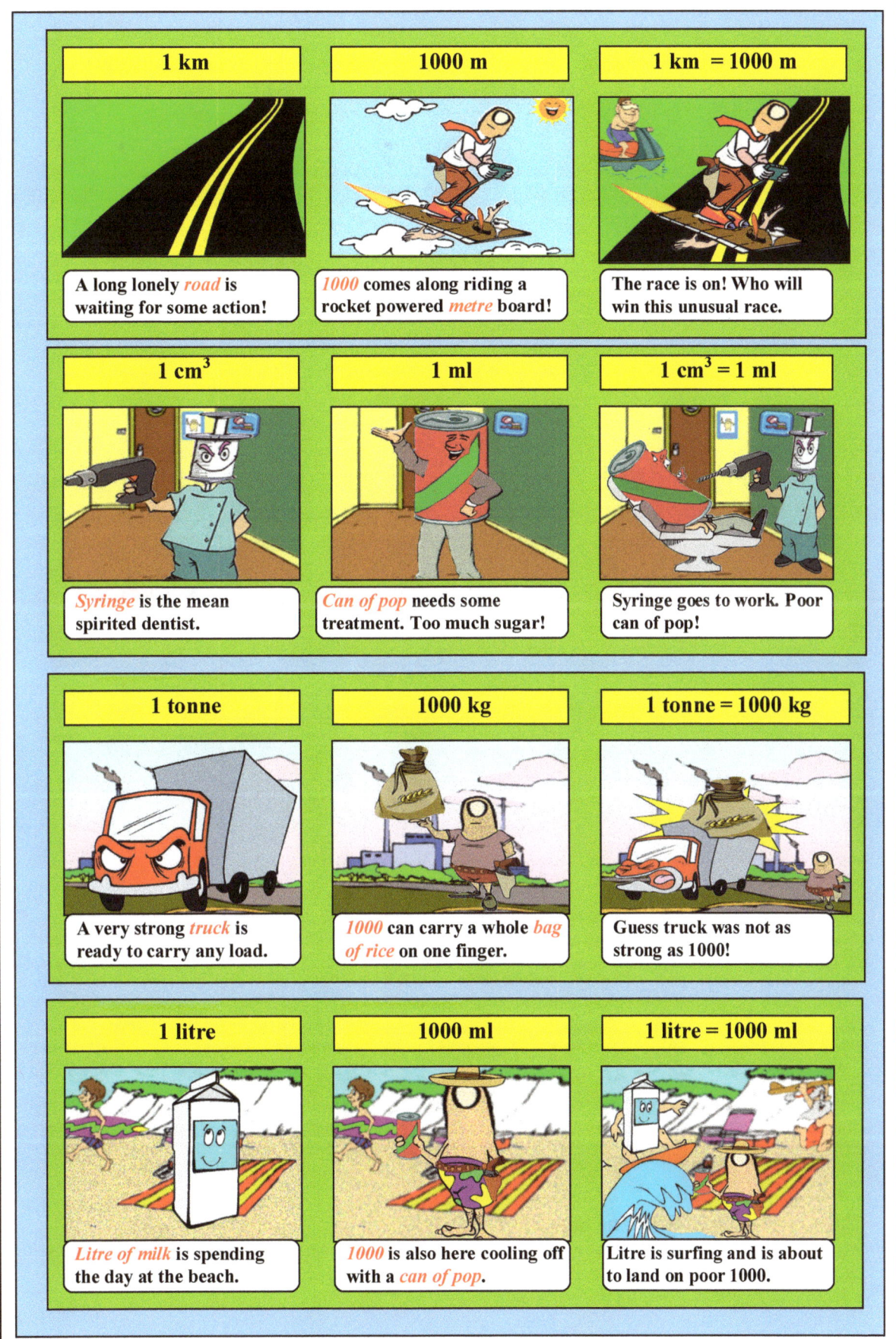

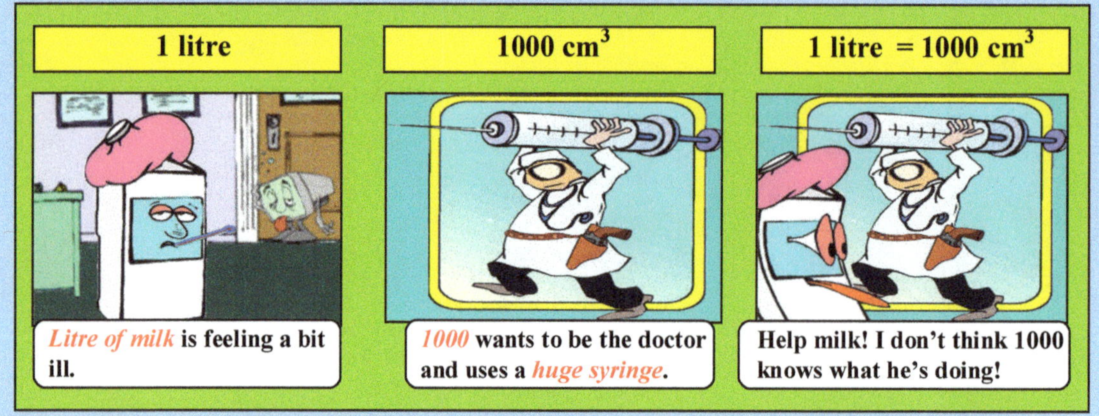

| 1 litre | 1000 cm³ | 1 litre = 1000 cm³ |

Litre of milk is feeling a bit ill.

1000 wants to be the doctor and uses a *huge syringe*.

Help milk! I don't think 1000 knows what he's doing!

| 1 kg | 1000 g | 1 kg = 1000 g |

A *bag of rice* is part of the shopping goods.

1000 is a robber who sneaks up on *gran*!

Bet he never expected this. Gran's hits him with the rice!

Here are a few Imperial Units:

- Length → Inches, feet, yards, miles
- Area → Square inches, square feet, Square yards, square miles
- Volume → Cubic inches, cubic feet, gallons, pints
- Weight → Ounces, pounds, stones, tons
- Speed → mph

The **conversion factors** for these are:
1 Foot = 12 inches
1 Yard = 3 Feet
1 Gallon = 8 Pints
1 Stone = 14 pounds(lbs)
1 pound = 16 Ounces(Oz)

Challenge!

Now that the more difficult metric units have been done for you, have a go at creating stories for the imperial units.

Cool Fact: The International System of Units (abbreviated SI) is the modern form of the metric system. It is the world's most widely used system of units.

You have a go:
1000 m = 1km. How many kilometres is 6767 metres?

The Number line

Think of a slide with numbers on them. Our numbers get *smaller as they slide down the line.*

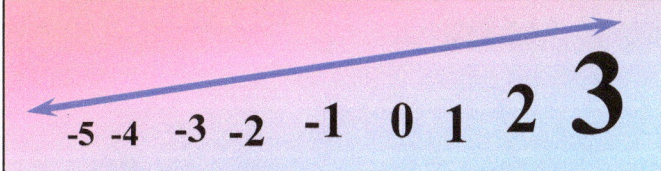

← Gets *smaller* as we move to the **Left**

→ Gets *larger* as we move to the **Right**

Putting numbers in order.

Example: place the following numbers in order: 10 -4 9 -6 2 -5 8

Simply place the numbers in the *same order* as they appear on the *number line*.

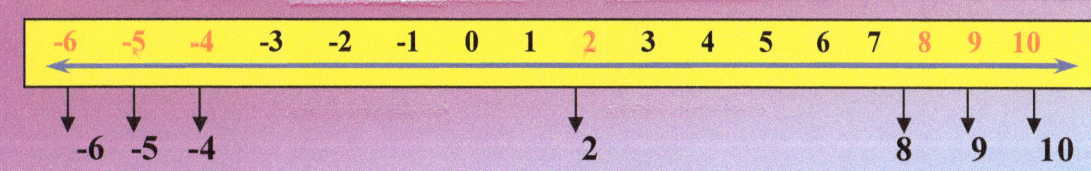

So the order is   -6 -5 -4 2 8 9 10. Remember: -6 is really smaller than -5. The further a number lies to the left, the smaller it is!

To be able to find a range of values.

Example: One day the temperatures in Johannesburg were $8\,^{0}C$ and $-2\,^{0}C$. What was the full *range* of temperature?

Just draw a number line and *find the numbers*. Then *count* the number of *spaces in between* the numbers.

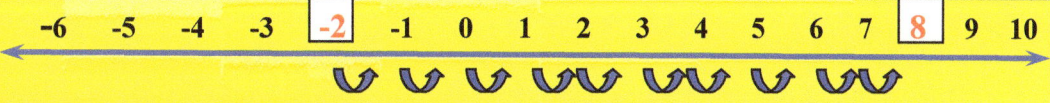

10 spaces

Answer: The full range of temperature in Johannesburg is $10\,^{0}C$.

Shortcut: Just add the two values while ignoring the negative sign: $8 + 2 = 10$

You could say : $8 - -2 = 10$

Copyright © Sunnil Singh 2008

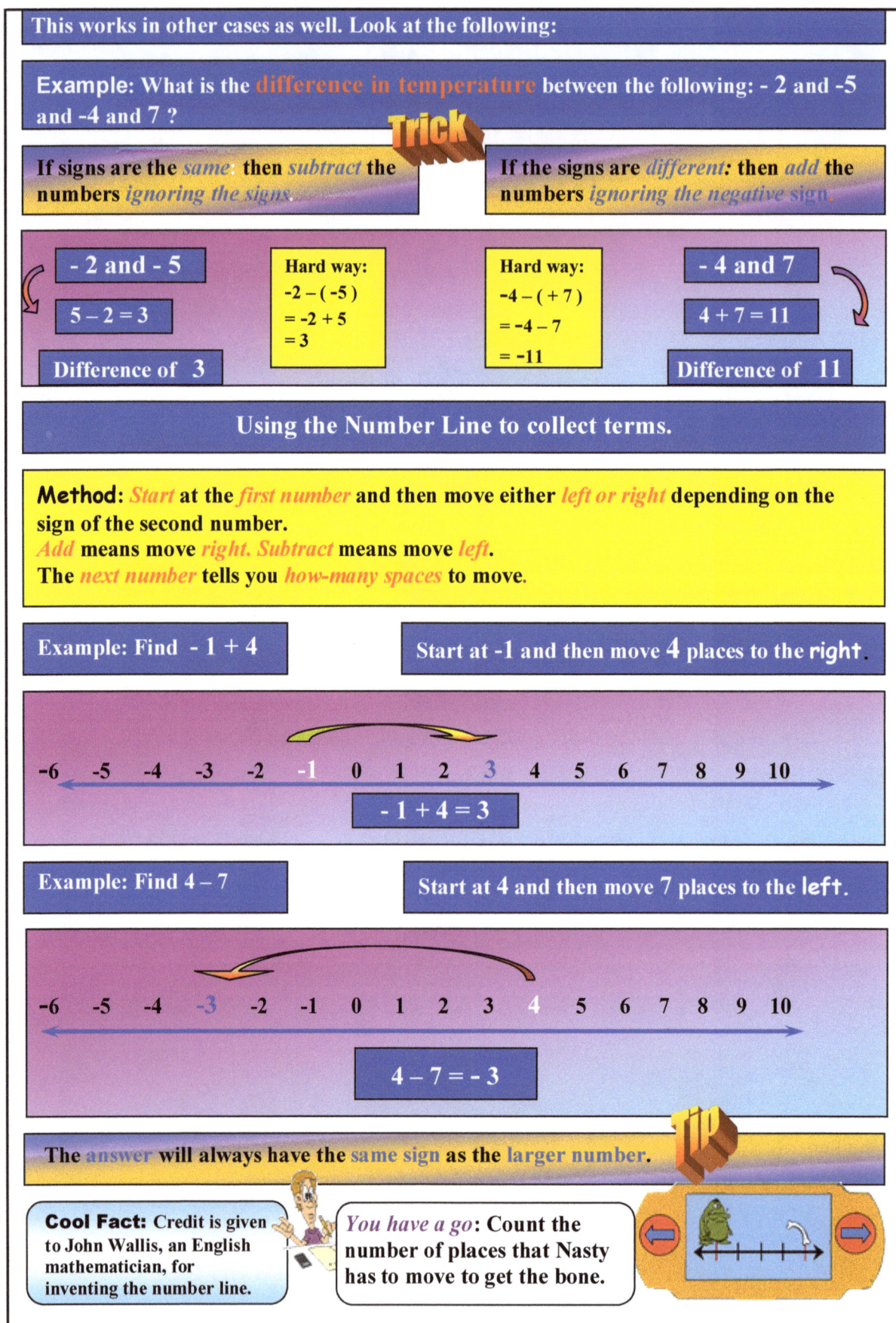

Negative Numbers

The word *negative* makes us think of someone who is *unhappy or grumpy*. Could you imagine anyone more grumpy or negative than our negative number character?

Rules for Multiplying and Dividing

These are the simple rules that will show you how to *divide or multiply negative* **numbers**:

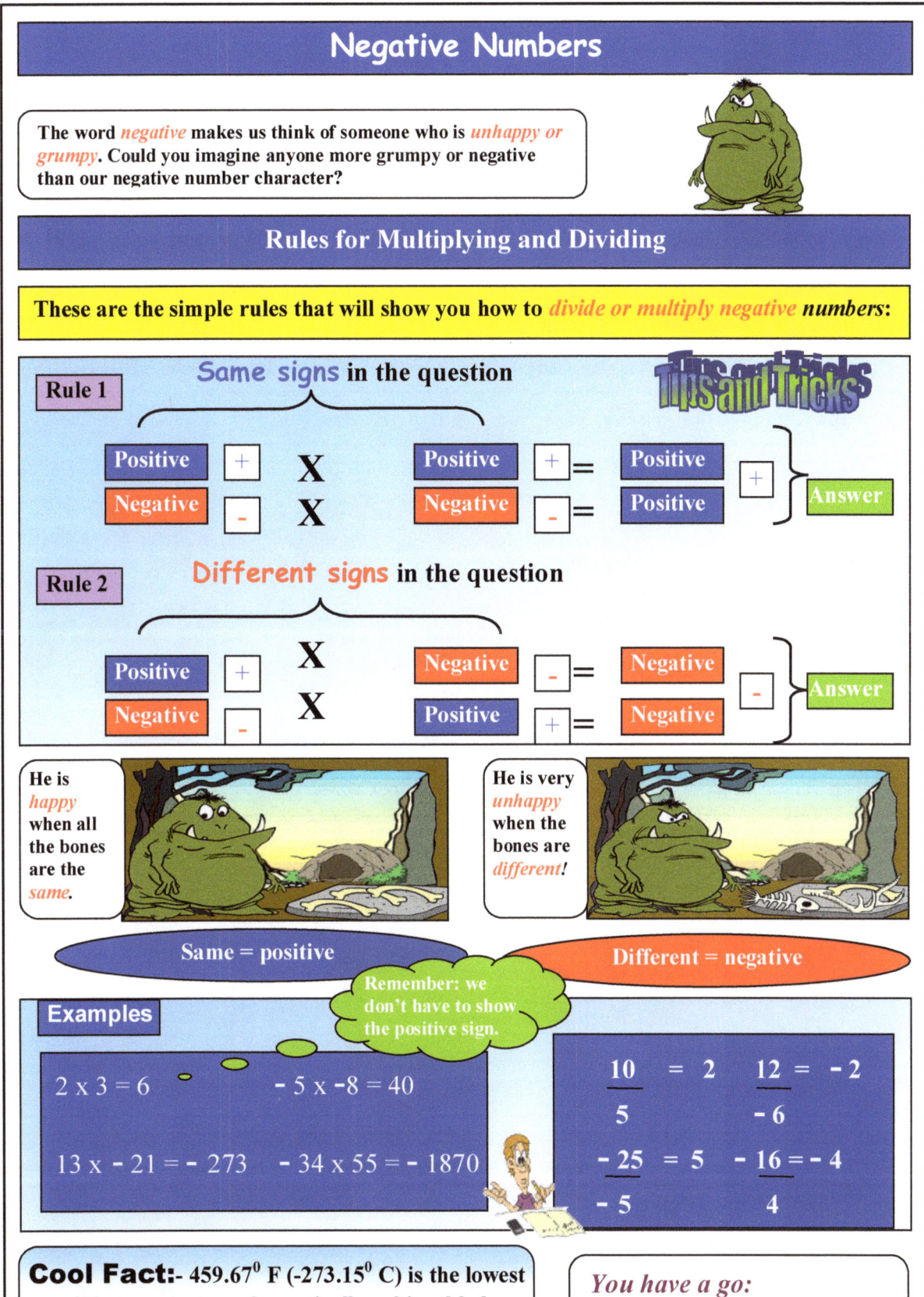

Rule 1 — Same signs in the question:
- Positive (+) × Positive (+) = Positive (+)
- Negative (−) × Negative (−) = Positive (+)
→ Answer: +

Rule 2 — Different signs in the question:
- Positive (+) × Negative (−) = Negative (−)
- Negative (−) × Positive (+) = Negative (−)
→ Answer: −

He is *happy* when all the bones are the *same*.

He is very *unhappy* when the bones are *different*!

Same = positive   **Different = negative**

Remember: we don't have to show the positive sign.

Examples

$2 \times 3 = 6$ $-5 \times -8 = 40$

$13 \times -21 = -273$ $-34 \times 55 = -1870$

$$\frac{10}{5} = 2 \quad \frac{12}{-6} = -2$$

$$\frac{-25}{-5} = 5 \quad \frac{-16}{4} = -4$$

Cool Fact: -459.67° F (-273.15° C) is the lowest possible temperature theoretically achievable by a system. Normally referred to as *Absolute Zero*.

You have a go:
Multiply:
a) 12×-7 b) -4×-8

Ordering Decimals

Sounds like deci-mole so picture our mole character!

Our decimole character is being ordered around by another nasty decimole with a gun!

Follow these few easy steps to arrange decimals: **Example:** arrange the following numbers from **smallest to largest**. 0.55   0.089   1.597   0.02584   0.4181

Step 1: Arrange the numbers in *columns* with the *decimal points* *one below the other*.

Decimal points ↓

0.55
0.089
1.597
0.02584
0.4181

The nasty decimole then makes the others perform circus tricks by balancing *one-on-top of another! (Columns)*. They wear the decimal points as belt buckles.

Step 2: Make them all the *same length*. Just fill in *extra zeros*.

Decimal points ↓

0.55000
0.08900
1.59700
0.02584
0.41810

A circus performer now passes them *circular hoops (zeros)*, which they have to balance.

Step 3: *Ignore* the *decimal points* and *the zeros at the front*. Now treat as *whole numbers*.

55000
8900
159700
2584
41810

A nasty decimole *sucks out the decimal points and zeros* with a plunger! All their clothes then fall off.

Step 4: Arrange in *order.*

2584
89**00**
4181**0**
55**000**
1597**00**

The ringmaster *arranges these naked decimoles in order.* Who's the boy at the back?

Step 5: *Put back* all the *decimal points* and *zeros* that were *there before.*

0.02584
0.089
0.4181
0.55
1.597

Finally a kind decimole *gives back* all their clothes, decimal points and zeros!

Cool Fact

Five hundred years after the introduction of decimal notation there is still no agreed symbol for the decimal divider or 'point'. The modern tradition in English-speaking countries is to use the full stop (.), while Europe generally uses the comma (,).

You have a go:
**Arrange the following decimals in descending order (highest to lowest):
0.1 , 2.5 , 0.098 , 0.978 , 1.97**

Percentages

Sounds similar to: Pear-cent-age. So picture a pear with a coin on his head!

Remember: 100 is a gun dressed as a hunter.

Percentages are *numbers out of* **or** *over* **100.**
Therefore, 35% = $^{35}/_{100}$ (35 ÷ 100).

20% = $^{20}/_{100}$ = 0.2   5% = $^{5}/_{100}$

89% = $^{89}/_{100}$ 14.4% = $^{14.4}/_{100}$

Percent character thinks that he can ride 100 as a horse at the rodeo. We see him *over or on top off 100*.

Type one: Work out percentages *of* an *amount*.

Multiplication comes along and tries to lasso percentage.

"of" means "x" in maths.

We use the multiplication character since "x" means "times".

Example: Find 20% of £60.

Answer:

With a calculator: 0.2 x 60 = £12

20%	of	60
$^{20}/_{100}$	X	60

20 divided by 100.

Without a calculator:
$^{20}/_{100} = ^{1}/_{5}$
Refer to simplifying fractions. Divide top and bottom by largest number. Here it is 20 that divides into both.

To find a fraction of an amount just divide by the denominator.
$^{1}/_{5}$ of 60 = 60 ÷ 5 = £12

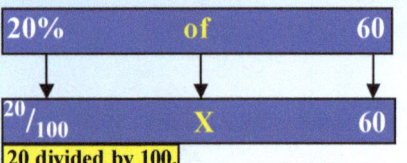

Type Two: Percentage *Decrease*.

Here we *take away* the percentage from the original amount.

Subtraction cuts in on the action and tries to *take away* percentage. He manages to pull him off but this only makes multiplication angry.

Example: In a sale the price of a dress costing £21 has been *reduced by* 10%. What is the new selling price?
Answer: 10% of £21 = 0.1 x £21 = £2.10. *Reduced by means to take away*. So the new selling price: £21 - £2.10 = £18.90

Type Three: Percentage *Increase*.

Here we *add on* the percentage to the original amount.

Addition tries to help Percentage and *adds him* back onto 100 using his crane!

Example: The price of a new pair of trainers that was £13 has *increased by* 20%. What is the new selling price? (Note: 20% = 0.2)

Answer:
20% of £13 = 0.2 x £13 = £2.60
Increase means to add on, so the new price is £13 + £2.60 = £15.60

This could also have been done using a **Multiplier**. £13 x 1.2 = £15.60

The multiplier used was **1.2**

This represents *one whole*. Always use one here.

Remember:
20% = 0.2
so 1 + 0.2 = 1.2

This represents the percentage (previously added on).

Look at the following: Increase an amount by the following percentages:

Percentage	30%	45%	66%	2%	17.5%
Multiplier to use	1.3	1.45	1.66	1.02	1.175

Another example: The final price of my new portable stereo costing £233 must include a 17.5% vat charge. What do I pay for the stereo?
Answer: £233 x 1.175 = £273.76

Type Four: Expressing *one number* as a *percentage of another.*

First write it as a ➡ **fraction** then as a ➡ **decimal** then as a ➡ **percentage**.
(Smaller number over larger)   just divide   x by 100

Example: 21 out of the 34 children in a class passed their maths test. What is this as a percentage?

Answer $^{21}/_{34}$ ➡ 0.62 ➡ 62%
(Rounded to 2dp)

Cool Fact
The earth is made up of 71% water while our bodies are made up of almost 70% water.

You have ago: An mp3 player is priced at £35 but there is a 15% discount. Find out how much you will save with the discount and how much the mp3 player will then cost?

Prime Numbers

Think of a *prime* piece of meat!

A **Prime Number** does *not divide* by anything.

Example: 12 is not a prime number since 1,2,3,4,6 and 12 will go into it exactly.

Prime is asleep while *division* prepares to go to work!

Although division tries, he *cannot divide* up prime.

However, only *1* and the *number itself* will *divide* into a prime number exactly.

Example: 7 is a prime number since only 1 and 7 can go into it exactly.
5 is a prime number since only 1 and 5 can go into it exactly.

Now a copy of *himself* and *a gun* do manage to divide him up. What a nightmare!

Prime awakes from the nightmare. Boy is he relieved.

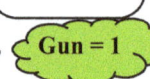

Gun = 1

You can also say that a prime number *has only two factors*: **1 × itself**
Example: only **1 x 7 = 7** or only **1 x 5 = 5**. Look at these prime numbers:

| 2 | 3 | 5 | 7 | 11 | 13 | 17 | 19 | 23 | 29 | 31 | ... |

Take note of the following;
  a) 1 *is not* a prime number.
  b) 2 and 5 are *exceptions* because all the others end in 1, 3, 7 or 9.
  c) Not all numbers ending in 1, 3, 7 or 9 are primes: example 21, 33, 57 etc.

To find a prime number

Example: Find all prime numbers between say 30 and 40.

Remember: they end in 1, 3, 7, or 9

First: the only possible answers are 31, 33, 37 and 39.
Second: divide each number by 3 and 7. If they divide exactly they are **not primes.**

33 ÷ 3 = 11 and 39 ÷ 3 = 13   Divide exactly (therefore **not primes**).
Answer: prime numbers between 30 and 40 are **31** and **37**

They all **end in 1, 3, 7 or 9**   Continue our story from here in order to remember this.

Remember: 1 = gun   3 = tree   7 = heaven   9 = line

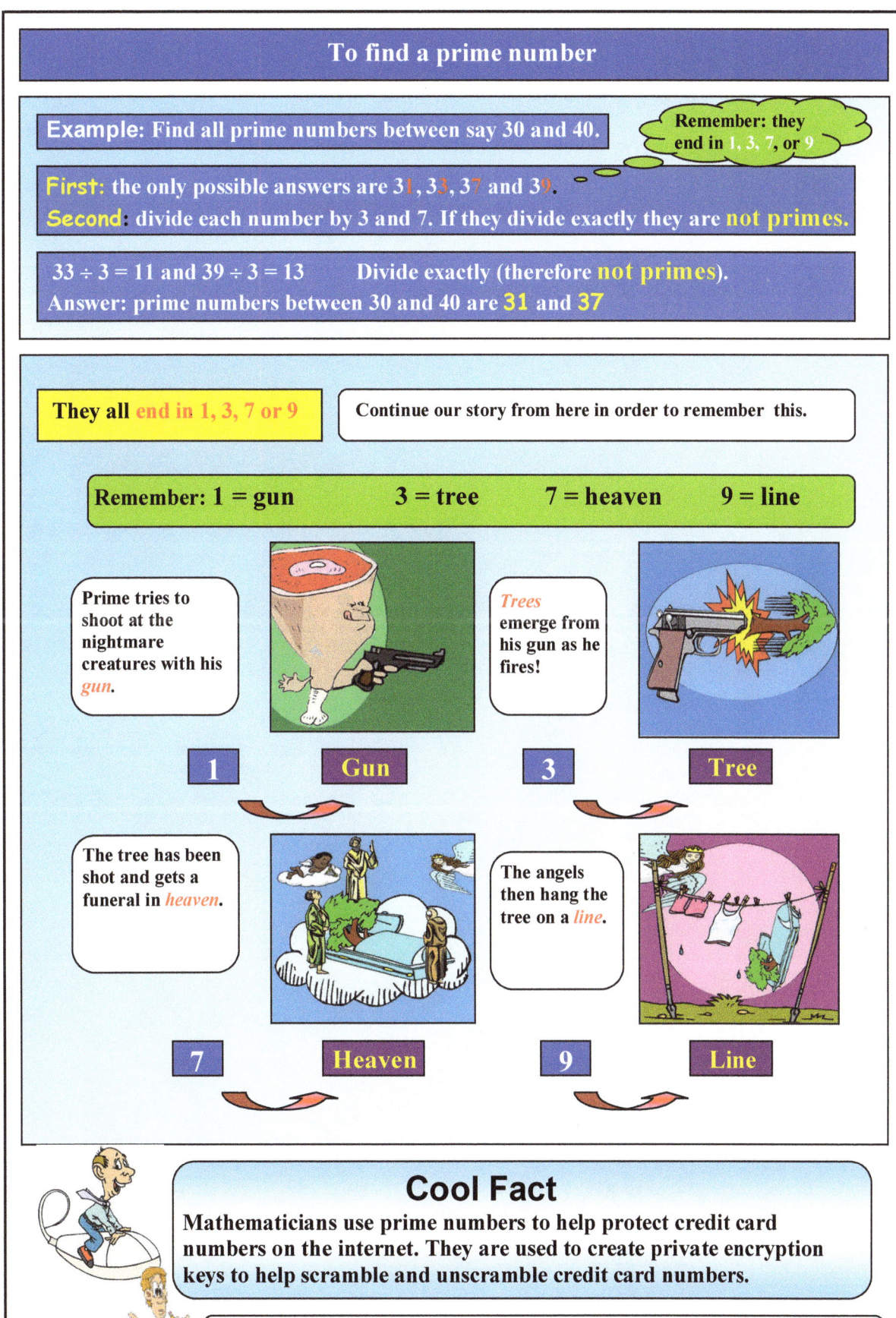

Prime tries to shoot at the nightmare creatures with his *gun*.

1 — Gun

Trees emerge from his gun as he fires!

3 — Tree

The tree has been shot and gets a funeral in *heaven*.

7 — Heaven

The angels then hang the tree on a *line*.

9 — Line

Cool Fact

Mathematicians use prime numbers to help protect credit card numbers on the internet. They are used to create private encryption keys to help scramble and unscramble credit card numbers.

You have a go: Find all the prime numbers between 80 and 100!

Ratio

Sounds like ray-show. So we picture a stingray conducting a show or ceremony!

A ratio is simply a way of *relating one number to another* in some meaningful way.

Ratio conducts a wedding ceremony where one person is *related to another in some meaningful way.*

Example: the ratio 2:3 (read as '2 is to 3'), could mean any one of a number of things
- 2 parts squash mixed with 3 parts water to make juice
- 2 parts red paint mixed with 3 parts yellow paint
- for every 2 sweets I give you I keep 3 (sharing)

and so on...

We can use ratios to help us *increase or decrease amounts* in the correct way so that the *relationship* between the numbers *stays the same*.

Ratio uses his magic wand but accidentally *increases* the bride while *decreasing* the groom in size! Fortunately their love *stays the same.*

If I wanted to make **more juice**, but still have it taste right, then I would use the ratio 2:3 but just change each part of the ratio in the same way.
So if the ratio 2:3 serves say 6 people then for 12 people it would now be:

Squash : Water

(6 people) →×2→ (12 people)

2 : 3 →×2, ×2→ 4 : 6

Copyright © Sunnil Singh 2008

We can also use ratios to *share amounts* in different parts.

Ratio's magic seems to have driven the groom mad. He now wants to cut up and *share out* the bride into *different parts*!!!

This is called **Proportional Division**

Proportional Division

Example: I want to share my winnings of **£1200** in the ratio of **1:2:3** between my friends. (*I like some more than the others!*).

First: Find the *total number of shares*.

A rather nervous *addition* is asked to *add up all the shares* of the bride.

$1 + 2 + 3 = 6$ shares in total.

Second: Find out how many parts is be given for *1 share*.

The deranged groom appears with a *gun* determined not to let anyone steal his bride!

Just divide the value to be shared by the total shares. $1200 \div 6 = 200$ parts.

Third: Now *multiply* to get the amounts for each share.

Fortunately, *multiplication* is on hand to put the shares right and restore harmony!

1 share = £200 x **1** = £200
2 shares = £200 x **2** = £400
3 shares = £200 x **3** = £600
                                    £1200

Copyright © Sunnil Singh 2008

Remember the following: a **Ratio** is **Fraction** is a **Decimal**

You should be able to convert between them.
The ratio $3:6$ is the same as $3 \div 6$ or $\dfrac{3}{6} = \dfrac{1}{2}$ and also the same as 0.5

The **Golden Rule** for Fractions applies to ratios as well.

Whatever you do to one part, you do exactly the same to the other.

Example: Simplify $4:20$

Divide both sides by the **largest number** that fits exactly (in this example it is 4).

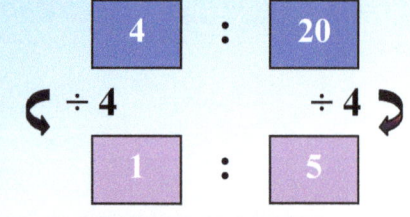

We do exactly the same on both sides.

Answer: 1 : 5

Example: Express $3:9$ as a fraction in its **simplest form**.

$3:9$ is the same as $\dfrac{3}{9}$ (Now simplify) $\dfrac{3 \div 3}{9 \div 3} = \dfrac{1}{3}$

We do exactly the same to the top and bottom.

Lastly, if you are given some **awkward looking ratio**, it is best to express it in the form $1 : n$ (n = any number).

Example: Simplify $9 : 87$

Simply *divide* both sides by the *smaller number*.

$9 : 87$
$\div 9 \quad \div 9$
Answer $1 : 9.6$

Cool fact
The golden ratio of 1.618 can be found in the arrangement of the whorls of a pine cone and even petals of a sunflower.

You have a go:
Simplify: a) 8:13
b) 5: 20

Rounding off

We use rounding off very often even when we are not aware of it.
At a **football match** we might just **estimate the number of people** that are present and give a figure of say 700. This is an estimate that has been **rounded off**. You will learn how to both estimate and round off values.

Picture someone playing **a round off** golf!

At a **supermarket** people will often **round off the values of items** and then add them up so that they have an idea of what it will cost when they get to the till. Rounding off prices makes it easier to add!

Basically we round off numbers to the number that they are closest to.

Rounding Off Whole Numbers

We round off numbers to the nearest **whole** number, nearest **ten**, nearest **hundred** and nearest **thousand**. There is an easy way to do this:

1. The number will always *lie between two possible answers*; just choose the one that it is *nearest to*.

Hint: Try to find the *half-way mark*

If the number is at or *above* the half-way mark, *round up*.

If the number is *below* the half-way mark, *round down*.

The following story will help us remember theses rules.

Our golfer has hit the ball. It **lies between two** holes. He tries to get it into the hole that it is **nearest to**.

Find the *half-way mark*.

Our frustrated golfer gets help from a teacher.

First she tells him to *find the half-way mark.*

> If the number is at or *above* the half-way mark, *round up*.
> If the number is *below* the half-way mark, *round down*

Examples: Round off each of the following: Just remember this diagram.

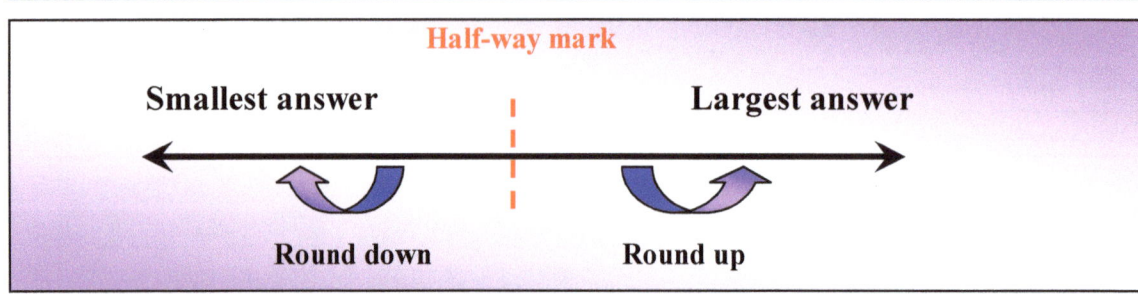

1. Give **89** to the nearest **ten**:
   Answer: 89 lies between 80 and 90 but is closer to 90 (above the half-way mark), so we **round up** to 90.

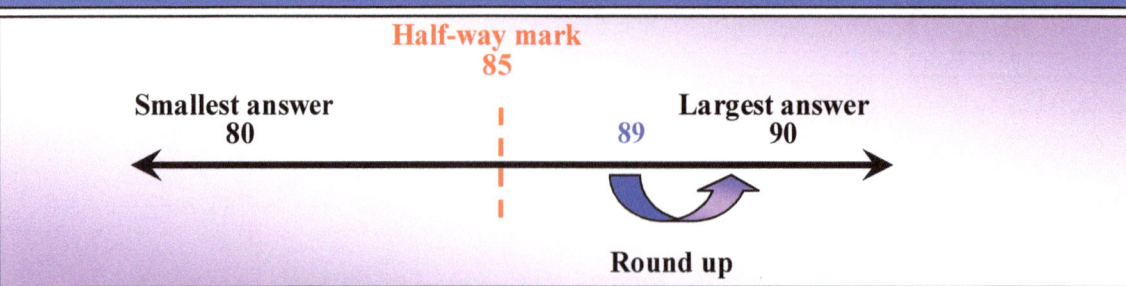

2. Give **144** to the nearest **ten**:
   Answer: 144 lies between 140 and 150 but is closer to 140 (below the half-way mark), so we **round down** to 140.

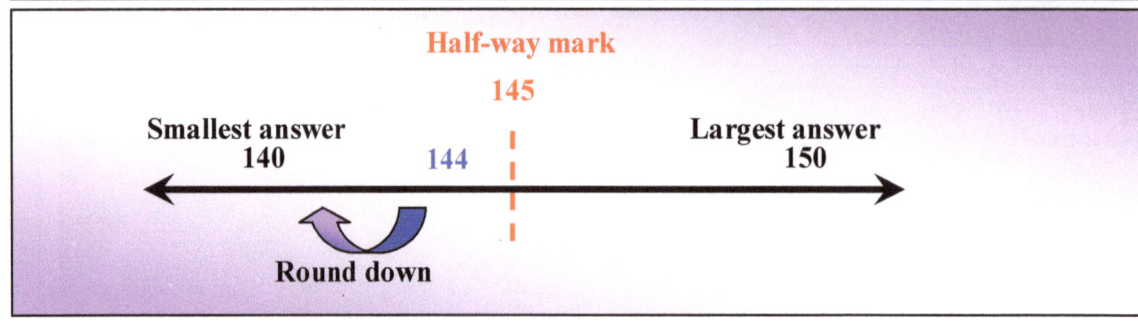

Copyright © Sunnil Singh 2008

3. Give **233** to the nearest **hundred**:
   Answer: 233 lies between 200 and 300 but is closer to 200(below the half-way mark), so we **round down** to 200.

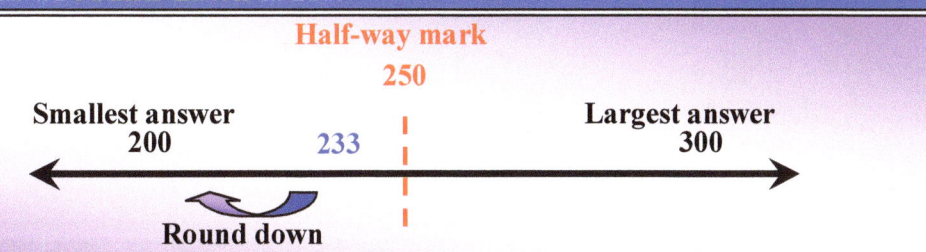

4. Give **1597** to the nearest **thousand**:
   Answer: 1597 lies between 1000 and 2000 but is closer to 2000(above the half-way mark), so we **round up** to 2000.

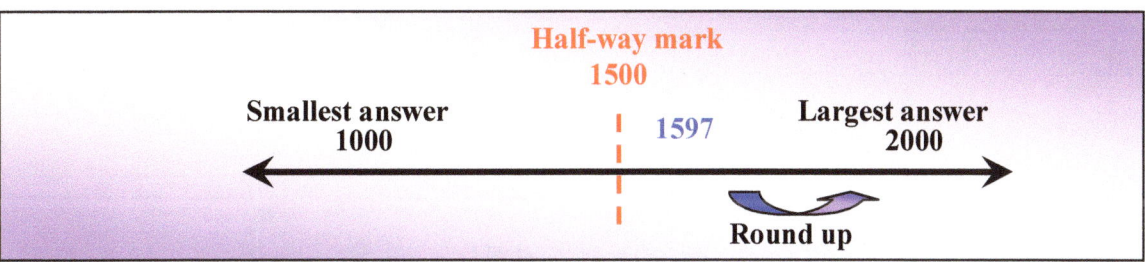

5. Give **34.6** to the nearest **whole number**:
   Answer: 34.6 lies between 34 and 35 but it is closer to 35(above the half-way mark), so we **round up** to 35.

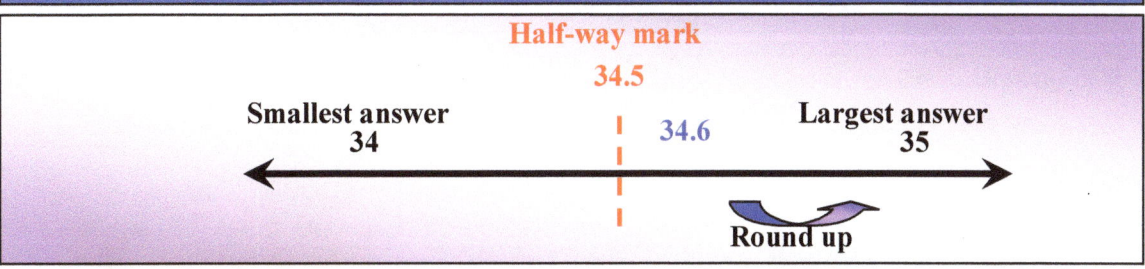

When the number is exactly in the **middle** (at the half-way mark), just **round up**.

Fortunately at last the flag lies exactly **in the middle**. Overjoyed he **flies up** using his jet powered golf bag!

Give **55** to the nearest **ten**: **Answer:** 55 is **exactly between** 50 and 60 so we **round up** to 60.

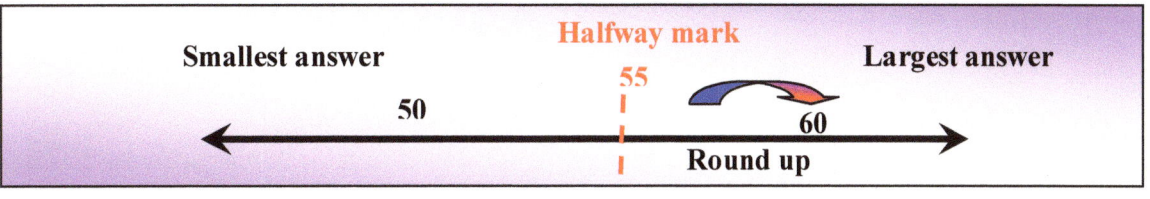

Copyright © Sunnil Singh 2008

Rounding off Decimals

"Digit sounds like midget so we will use midgets."

Decimole is overseeing some midgets playing a round of golf. It seems as though the midgets are unhappy about who has won!

Remember: Decimal place refers to the number of digits after the decimal point.

More decimal places mean more accurate answers.

- 5.8 → Number given with **one** decimal place
- 13.21 → Number given with **two** decimal places
- 2.358 → Number given with **three** decimal places

Identify the **last digit** based on the question.
13.**2**134 rounding to one decimal place: last digit = 2
13.2**1**34 rounding to two decimal places: last digit = 1

Now look at the digit to the right – called the **Decider**.

The competition was held to decide which *midget came last.*

A judge is called in to act as the *Decider* and to see if the correct midget won.

If the **Decider** is 5 or more, then round-up the **last digit**.   Remember: 5 = hive.
If the **Decider** is 4 or less, then leave the **last digit** as it is.   Remember: 4 = door.

The winner proves his worth by climbing up to the hive as directed by the judge.

Satisfied the judge leaves things unchanged and makes the winner stand by a door!

Example: Round 8.13 to **one** decimal place

$$8.1\mathbf{3} = 8.1$$

Since the Decider is less than 5, we leave the last digit the same.

Example: Round 610.987 to **two** decimal places.

$$610.9\mathbf{8}7 = 610.99$$

Since the Decider is more than 5, we round the last digit up to 9.

Significant Figures

Significant figures tell us how accurate we are being. The more significant figures, the more accurate. In any number the first significant figure is the first digit that is not a zero.

The first significant figure is shown in each of the numbers below:

0.0**3**77   **6**10
9.87   **1**597

Also note the following:

0 . **2** **5** **8** 4
    1st 2nd 3rd 4th
(significant figures)

Rounding to a given number of significant figure

Steps to follow:
First: find the number of significant figures based on the question.
Second: look at the first unwanted digit.
Third: if the first unwanted digit is 5 or more then add 1 to the last significant figure. If it is 4 or less then the last significant figure stays the same.
All the unwanted digits turn into zeros and in the case of a decimal number they fall away.

Example: round off the following as shown: The number of significant figures is shown in red. The unwanted digits are shown in blue.

34 to 1 sf = 30
55 to 1 sf = 60
0.**9**87 to 1 sf = 1.000 = 1
(8 changes 9 to a 10, so we carry over 1 ten.)
(Zeros at the end of a decimal number fall away.)

1.**5**97 to 2 sf = 1.600 = 1.6
2584 to 2 sf = 2600
4.181 to 2 sf = 4.200 = 4.2
6765 to 3 sf = 6770
0.**1**0946 to 3 sf = 0.109

The following table illustrates rounding off to different significant figures:

Number	1 significant figure	2 significant figures	3 significant figures	4 significant figures
0.75025	0.8	0.75	0.75	0.7503
1.21393	1	1.2	1.21	1.214
0.0196418	0.02	0.02	0.0196	0.01964

You have a go: Round off the following numbers:
a) 13 to the nearest 10   b) 55 to the nearest 100
c) 144 to the nearest 100   d) 4181 to the nearest 1000

Cool Fact: The longest river in the world is the Amazon, which is about 6500 km long.

Copyright © Sunnil Singh 2008

Estimating

E for eel

Sounds similar to: *es-tea-mate*

Eel is having tea with his mates!

When **estimating**, all you do is **round off the numbers**, to nice **easy numbers** and then work out the answer.

Eel and his friends decide to have a **round of** golf. They round up some **numbers** and use them as balls. This makes their game much **easier**!

Example: Estimate the value of **34 x 55**.

Answer: 34 **rounds down** to 30. 55 **rounds up** to 60
Now multiply these two answers: 30 x 60 = 1800
1800 is a good estimate or you could say approximate value to the question.

Remember the rules for rounding

Trick for multiplying multiples of 10: Simply move the zeros from the question to the answer and then multiply what's left!

Example: Without a calculator estimate the value of the following. Show all working.

Example: $\dfrac{14.4 + 23.3}{37.4}$

Remember: We are only getting estimates to the answers. Don't be concerned about the answers being wrong.

Remember rules for rounding!

$14.4 + 23.3$ → Round off as shown → $\dfrac{14 + 23}{37} = \dfrac{37}{37} = 1$

37.4 →

Cool Facts

Would you like to guess or **estimate** the mass of the earth? Scientists have worked it out to be around 5.97×10^{24} kg!!!

You have a go:
Estimate the value of
$\dfrac{59.8 + 40.4}{49.7}$

Copyright © Sunnil Singh 2008

Time

With time we naturally think of a **clock**.

Let us first look at a few basics:

am and pm

'am' means 'morning' and it goes from 12 midnight to 12 noon.
'pm' means 'afternoon and evening' and it goes from 12 noon to 12 midnight.

60 seconds = 1 minute	7 days = 1 week	When working with time
60 minutes = 1 hour	4 weeks = 1 month	**just break up the**
24 hours = 1 day	12 months = 1 year	**problem into smaller parts.**

Some people hate being woken up in the morning!  He gets rid of his **problem** (clock) by **breaking it up.**

Example 1: How long is it from **8:13 to 12:43**?
Solution: Just break up the problem into **smaller parts** and try to work with **whole hours** where possible.

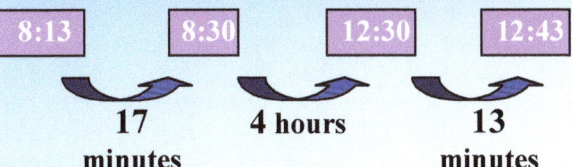

Now just add up the separate bits:
17 mins + 4 hours + 13 mins = **4 hours 30 mins.**

Example 2: A train leaves station A at **7:00 am** and travels for **3 hours 12 minutes** to station B. What time does it arrive at station B?
Solution: again just split up the problem into smaller parts.

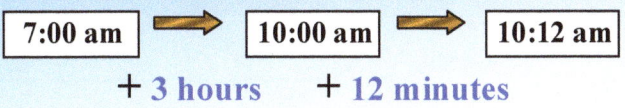

The train arrives at station B at 10:12 am.

Some questions on Time might use **calendars.**

First you need to remember the **number of days in each month.** Try this rhyme:

30 days hath September, April, June, and November.
All the rest have 31, except for February, which has 28.

Example 1: Ben worked 2 different jobs within the same year. One, from the 23rd of March to the 14th of April, and then again from the 5th of May to the 8th of September. How many days did he work altogether?

23 March 31	1 April 14	5 May 31	1 June 30	1 July 31	1 August 31	1 September 8
9 days	14 days	26 days	30 days	31 days	31 days	8 days

Add the bits together: 9+14+26+30+31+31+8 = 149 days.

Example 2: How many days are there from January 2nd 2006 to February 24th 2006?

2006	January					February			
Monday	2	9	16	23	30	6	13	20	27
Tuesday	3	10	17	24	31	7	14	21	28
Wednesday	4	11	18	25		1	8	15	22
Thursday	5	12	19	26		2	9	16	23
Friday	6	13	20	27		3	10	17	24
Saturday	7	14	21	28		4	11	18	25
Sunday	1	8	15	22	29	5	12	19	26

Solution:

January 2nd ➡ January 31st ➡ February 24th

30 days   24 days

Add these together: 30+24 = **54 days**

Cool Facts

One picosecond(1-trillionth of a second) is about the shortest period of time we can currently measure accurately!
1 centisecond(1-hundredth of a second),the length of time it takes for a stroke of lightening to strike!

You have a go: A train leaves London at 11:35 and travels to Manchester. The journey takes 11/2 hours. What time does it get to Manchester?

Some tricks with multiplication and division.

Alternate method of multiplication: Chinese multiplication

Could you multiply **89** by **144** or 144 by 233 without a calculator? Sure it could be done but not very easily! However, try this method:

Example: multiply **89** by **144**

Step 1: Arrange the numbers in a grid. For a 2 digit x 3 digit question you need a 2 by 3 grid and so on. Arrange the numbers along the top and side as shown:

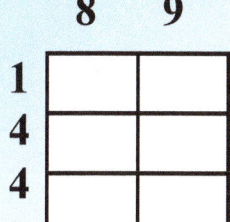
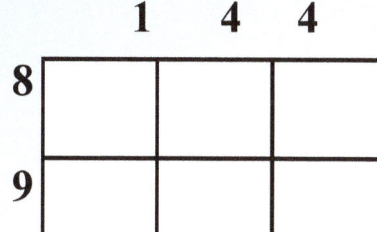

Note: the order does not matter. You could have done it either way.

Step 2: Now draw in diagonals in each box.

Step 3: Then cross multiply.

8 x 4 = 32

Write every answer as a two digit number therefore 9 is 0 9.

Step 4: Now add diagonally as shown by the green lines.

2 + 3 + 6 = 11
(Write down 1 and carry 1 to the next column)

Answer = 12816

To read off the answer just start with the diagonal on the left and work your way to the right!

Cool Fact: Evidence of multiplication tables date back to as long ago as 2000 BC.

You have a go:
Multiply: 233 x 377.

Copyright © Sunnil Singh 2008

Patterns in numbers

9 Times Table

4 − 1 = 3

9	x	1	=	0	+ 9
9	x	2	=	1	+ 8 = 9
9	x	3	=	2	+ 7
9	x	**4**	=	**3**	+ 6
9	x	5	=	4	+ 5
9	x	6	=	5	+ 4
9	x	7	=	6	+ 3
9	x	8	=	7	+ 2
9	x	9	=	8	+ 1
9	x	10	=	9	+ 0
9	x	11	=	9	+ 9
9	x	12	=	10	+ 8

The answer always starts with **one less** than the question.

Notice how the two digits of the answer always add up to one. 1 + 8 = 9

This pattern continues up to here.

Here we **repeat the digits**.

Here 1 + 8 = 9 with a zero in between.

Another tip: one easy way to write out your 9 times table would be to draw 2 columns first **going down from 0-9** the second **coming up from 0-9**.

So how do we use these patterns?

Say you were asked   9 x 7 = ?

Solution
        9   x   7   =   6 ?   The first digit is one less.

then
        9   x   7   =   6 + 3 = 9
                                    The next digit has to be 3 to add up to 9.

Answer: 63

Cool fact

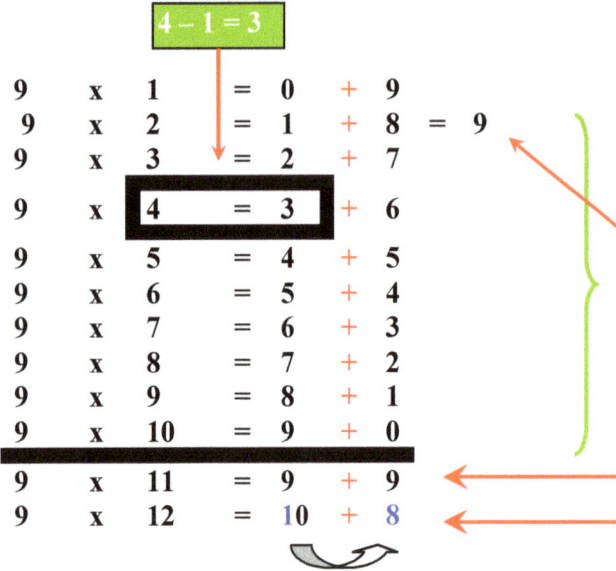

There are nine provinces in South Africa. Northern Cape, Eastern Cape, Western Cape, Kwa Zulu Natal, Free State, North-west province, Gauteng, Limpopo and Mpumalanga.

You have a go:

A teacher tells her pupils: Think of a number between 1 and 10. Multiply your number by nine, then add the digits of the answer, and then subtract 5. Use the code A=1, B=2, etc. to change your answer to a letter. Think of a country beginning with your letter. The teacher tells the pupils that the name of their country starts with the letter D! *The pupils are amazed!* Can you think of a mathematical reason as to why this trick works?

11 times table

11	x	1	=	11
11	x	2	=	22
11	x	3	=	33
.				
.				
.				
11	x	10	=	110
11	x	11	=	121
11	x	12	=	132

Notice how the digits of the answer are repeated from the question.

Always add a zero to whole numbers when multiplying by 10.

Add the two digits of the question to get the middle digit of the answer..

The numbers 1, 2, 3 rearranged.

Notice a very **useful pattern** that emerges from the last few multiplications!

Just **add** the **two digits of the question** to get the **middle digit** of the **answer**.

Example: 11 x 34

11 x   3 + 4   =   3 7 4   Answer

However, if the **sum** of the two digits is **more than nine**, you will have to **carry over to the next column**!

Example: 11 x 89

11 x   8 + 9   =   8 17 9

Write down the 7 and carry over the 1.

9 7 9   Answer

12 Times Table

12	x	1	=	12
12	x	2	=	24
12	x	3	=	36
12	x	4	=	48
12	x	5	=	60
12	x	6	=	72
12	x	7	=	84
12	x	8	=	96
12	x	9	=	108
12	x	10	=	120
12	x	11	=	132
12	x	12	=	144

Answer begins with the **same digit** as the question.

Answer begins with **one more** than the question.

Answer begins with **two more** than the question.

The last digits of the answer follow the **two times table**.

Cool fact
The twelve signs of the Zodiac are:
Aries, Taurus, Gemini, Cancer, Leo, Virgo, Libra, Scorpio, Sagittarius, Capricorn, Aquarius and Pisces.

Divisibility by 3 and 9

A number is divisible by 3 if the sum of it's digits is divisible by 3.

Example: $^{96}/_3$ = 32 since 9+6= 15
(Divisible by 3)

A number is divisible by 9 if the sum of it's digits is divisible by 9.

Example: $^{126}/_9$ = 14 since 1+2+6 =9
(Divisible by 9)

Cool fact: The three basic earth divisions are the: Core, Mantle and Crust.

Copyright © Sunnil Singh 2008

Division by 11

How can we tell if a number can be divided by 11?
Follow these easy steps:

First: Put alternate + and - signs in front of the digits.
Second: Total them up
Third: If the total is zero or it divides by 11, then the original number can be divided by 11.

Example: will 1453474 divide by 11?

Put alternate + and – signs in front of the digits.
+ 1 – 4 + 5 – 3 + 4 – 7 + 4

Then group together positive and negative parts and find the total.
+ 1 + 5 + 4 + 4 = + 14   - 4 – 3 – 7 = - 14
Since + 14 – 14 = 0 it will divide by 11.

Let's try another example:
What about 70752?

Put alternate + and – signs in front of the digits.
+ 7 – 0 + 7 – 5 + 2

Then group together positive and negative parts and find the total.
+ 7 + 7 + 2 = + 16   - 0 – 5 = - 5
Since + 16 – 5 = + 11 it will divide by 11.

Cool fact

Division by 11 is used to check if the ISBN in books is correct when fed into a computer!
The computer multiplies each digit by it's position and adds up the results. If this answer is divisible by 11 then the correct ISBN was used!

Multiplying and Dividing by 10, 100 and 1000 etc.

Multiplying by 10, 100, 1000

Multiplying means that your answer will get bigger. However if you multiply by decimals then your answer will get smaller!

We could do one of two things when multiplying by 10, 100 or 1000.

With whole numbers:
Add zeros to get the answer.
We add as many zeros as there are in the question.

Example:
58 x 10 = 580 (multiply by 10 so add 1 zero)
813 x 100 = 81 300 (multiply by 100 so add 2 zero)
5589 x 1000 = 5 589 000 (multiply by 1000 so add 3 zeros)

With decimals:
Move the decimal point to the right (note, strictly speaking the decimal point cannot move, the numbers do but it is easier to understand multiplication as being associated with the number line where *moving to the right means getting bigger*).

Gets smaller as we move to the Left

Gets larger as we move to the Right

-5 -4 -3 -2 -1 0 1 2 3

Example: 2 1 . 3 4 x 10 = 213.4
Move 1 place to the right.

Example: 8 . 1 3 x 100 = 813.0 = 813
Move 2 places to the right.

Example: 0 . 1 4 4 2 3 x 1000 = 144.23
Move 3 places to the right.

If there are no more spaces to jump just add zeros.
8.13 x 1000 = 8130
21.34 x 1000 = 21340

Remember this special number line:

÷ (division)   X (multiplication)

Smaller   Larger

Copyright © Sunnil Singh 2008

Dividing by 10, 100, 1000 etc.

If we keep the number line in mind and the rule about moving the decimal point then division is very easy! Remember **dividing means getting smaller** and so **we move to the left.**

Example: 5 8 ÷ 10 = 5.8
Move 1 place to the left.

Remember in any whole number the decimal point is sitting at the end of the number. Example **58.0 , 813.0 , 2134.0**

Example : 2 1 . 34 ÷ 10 = 2.134
Move 1 place to the left.

Example: 8 . 1 3 ÷ 100 = 0.0813
Move 2 places to the left.

Add zeros' into any gaps that you jump over and a zero before the decimal point.

Cool Facts (The number 10)
Pythagoreans regarded 10 as special number since it is the sum of the first four digits. In the United States, phone numbers are fixed-length, with a total of 10 digits. The 3-3-4 scheme, developed by AT&T in 1947, uses three blocks of numbers arranged in two blocks of three and a single block of four digits.

Cool Facts (The number 100)
It is the sum of the first nine prime numbers, as well as the sum of two prime numbers (47 + 53), and the sum of the cubes of the first four integers ($100 = 1^3 + 2^3 + 3^3 + 4^3$). Also, $2^6 + 6^2 = 100$, thus 100 is a Leyland number. Also:
- In Greece, India and Israel, 100 is the police telephone number.
- In Belgium, 100 is the ambulance telephone number.
- In the United Kingdom, 100 is the operator telephone number.

Cool Facts (The number 1000)
A millennium has 1000 years. The year 1000 is the last year of the first millennium AD. To count to one thousand, counting one number every second continuously would take about 16 minutes and 40 seconds.

You have a go: Take 163:
  a) Divide it by 10, 100 and then 1000.
  b) Multiply it by 10, 100 and then 1000.

Cool fact: When information travels from your computer along the internet, it is divided into data packets that can travel halfway across the world through several different networks and arrive at another computer in a fraction of a second!

Recap and Review of Number

 You were supposed to be doing your R and R!

 Oh! Thought you meant rest and relaxation!

1. When arranging numbers in order of size, what are the two steps involved?
2. Large numbers are always read in groups of three. True or false?
3. a) State 2 ways to find factors of a number.   b) List the first 8 factors of 144.
4. Fractions.
   a) Define a fraction.
   b) How can you tell the size of a fraction?
   c) What are equivalent fractions?
   d) What is the easiest way to simplify fractions?
   e) Convert $9\tfrac{8}{7}$ to an improper fraction.
5. List the conversion factors for a) metric units b) imperial units.
6. a) Numbers get larger as we move to the left on the number line. True or false?
   b) Which is smaller: -55 or 34 ?
7. a) When multiplying or dividing negative numbers what are the two simple rules or tricks that we should keep in mind?
   b) Simplify: - 144/ 89.
8. List in order the steps to be followed when ordering decimals.
9. Percentages.
   a) How would you define a percentage?
   b) What are the four kinds of problems that we generally get with percentages?
   c) Find 5% of £ 610.
10. Prime numbers.
    a) What is a prime number?
    b) Why are 2 and 5 exceptions?
    c) Is 1 a prime number?
    d) List all the prime numbers between 20 and 30.
11. Ratio
    a) Define a ratio?
    b) What is Proportional Division?
    c) List the steps involved in proportional division.
    d) Share £21 in the ratio 3:4
12. What is the golden rule that is used in both fractions and ratios?
13. Rounding.
    a) We round off numbers to the numbers that they are closest to. T or F?
    b) State the rules for rounding off whole numbers.
    c) State the rules for rounding off decimals.
14. How do we estimate?
15. How many seconds in a minute?

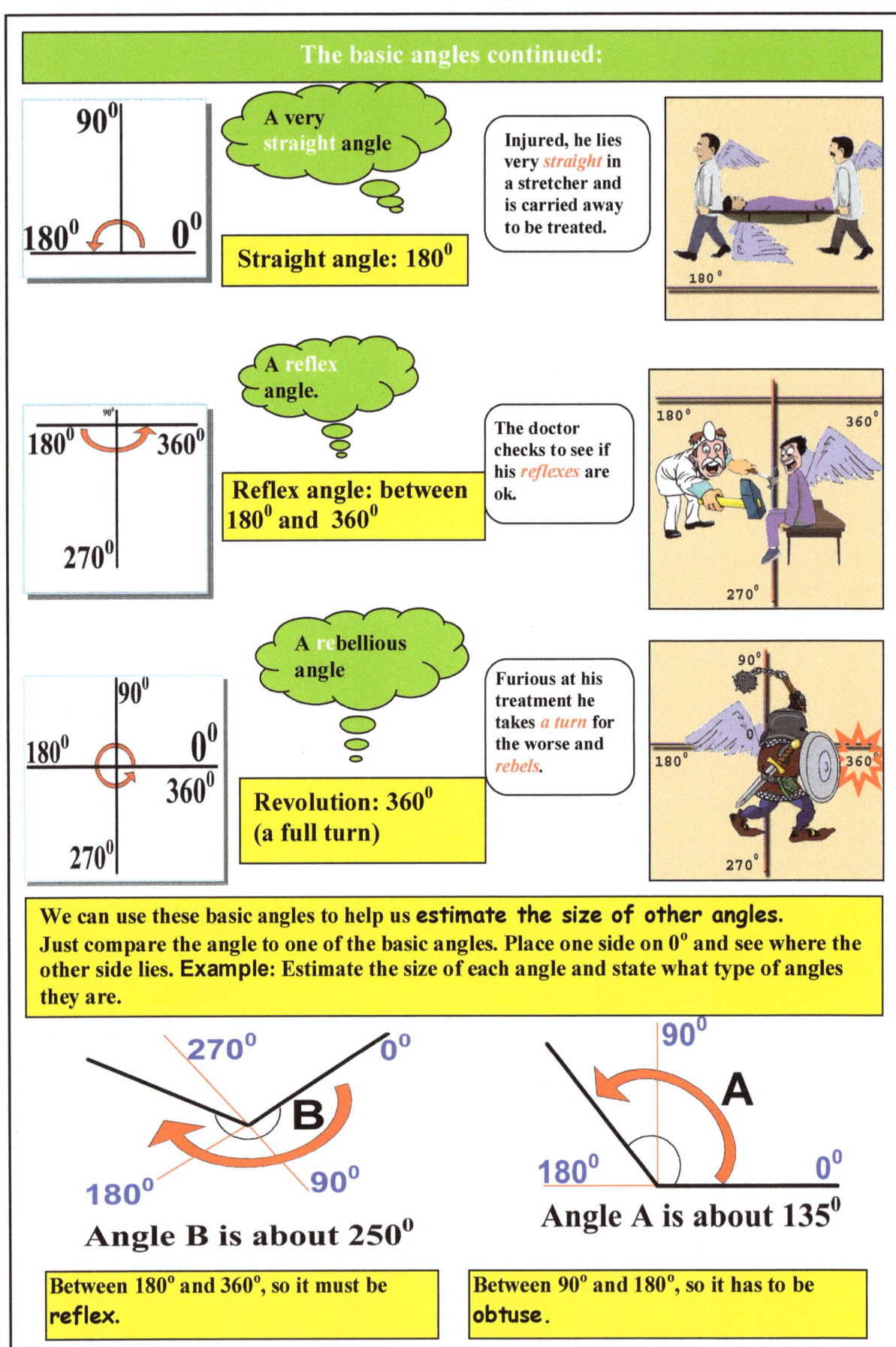

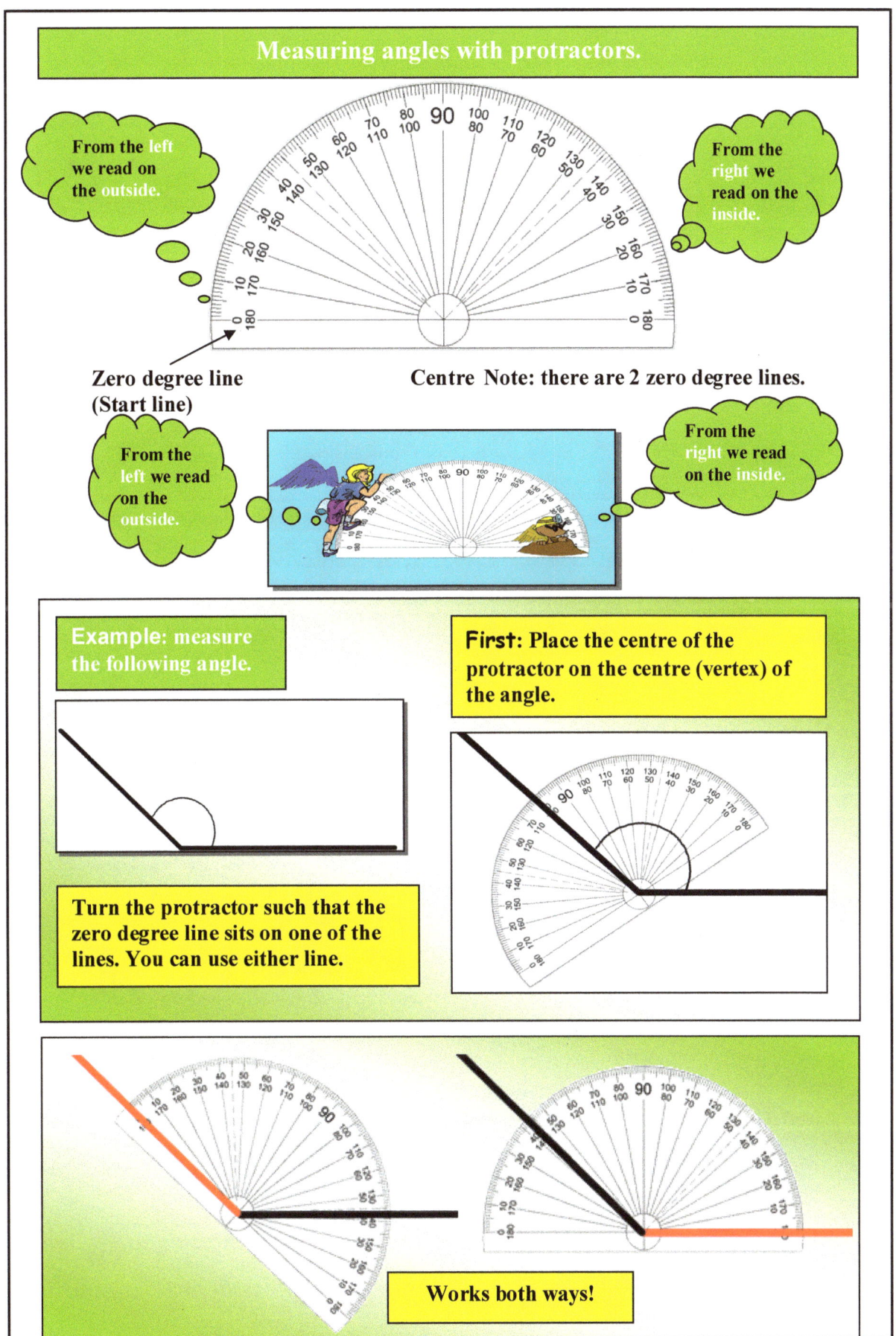

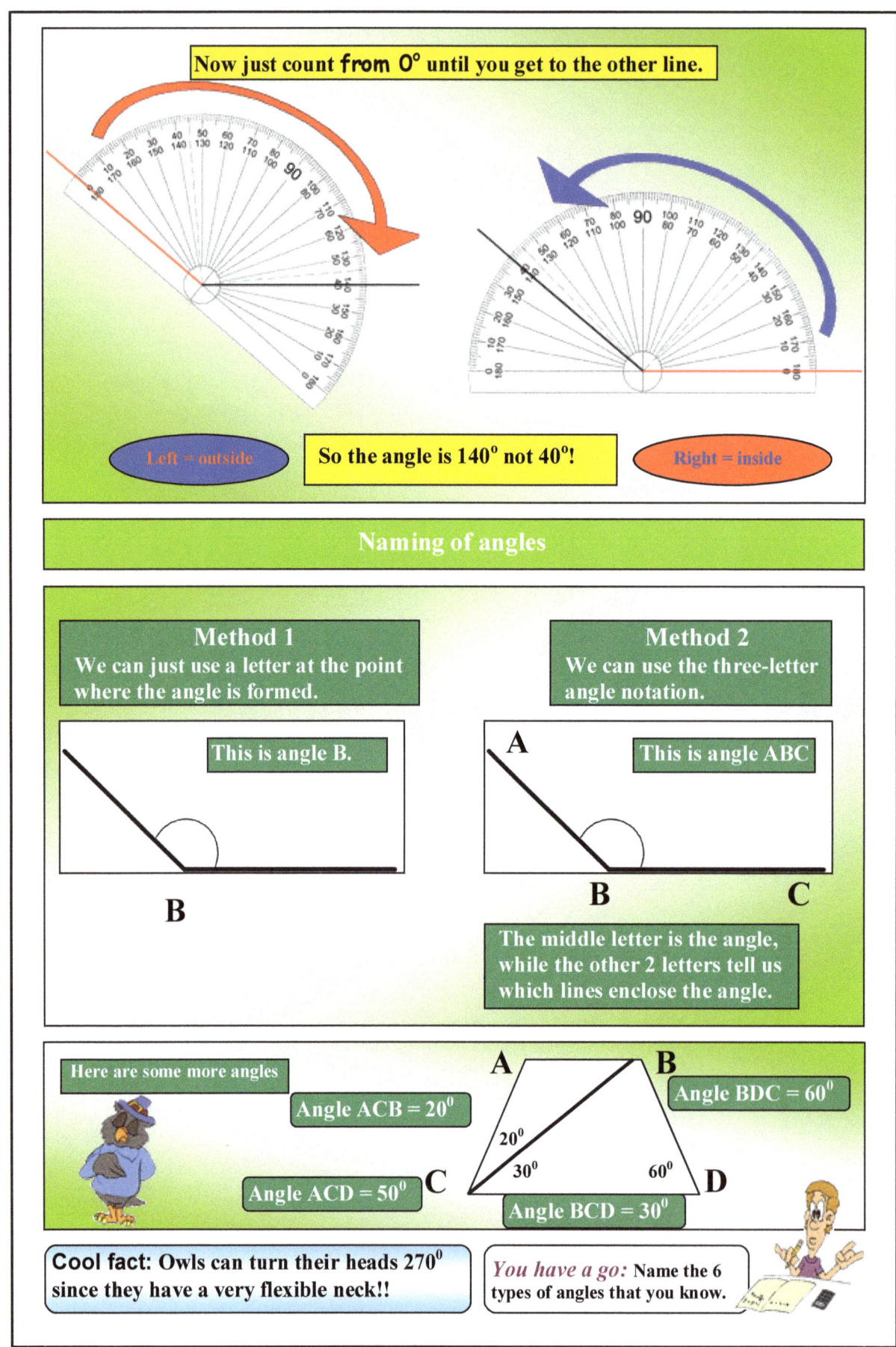

Angles and parallel lines.

Imagine an *angel* on a pair of *parallel bars*.

Whenever a line cuts across a pair of parallel lines two kinds of angles are formed: one *big* and one *small*.

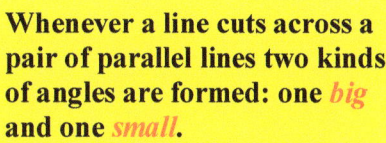

A line cuts the parallel bars using a giant pair of scissors.

Suddenly two angels emerge: *one small* and nasty, the *other large* and friendly.

The *big* angle and the *small* angle always add up to 180°.

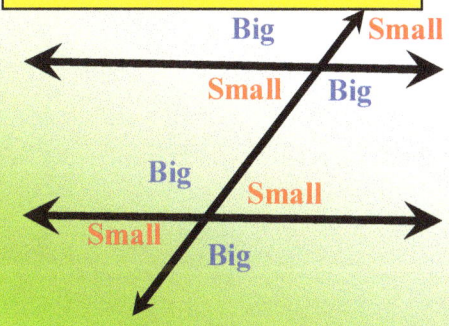

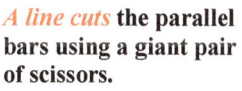

They fight each other but end up knocking each other out.

Both have to lie down *straight* on stretchers.

Many types of angles are formed when a pair of parallel lines are cut by a transversal.
Alternate angles: These are equal.

Supplementary angles: These add up to 180°.

Corresponding angles: These are equal.
We continue our story to help us remember these angles.

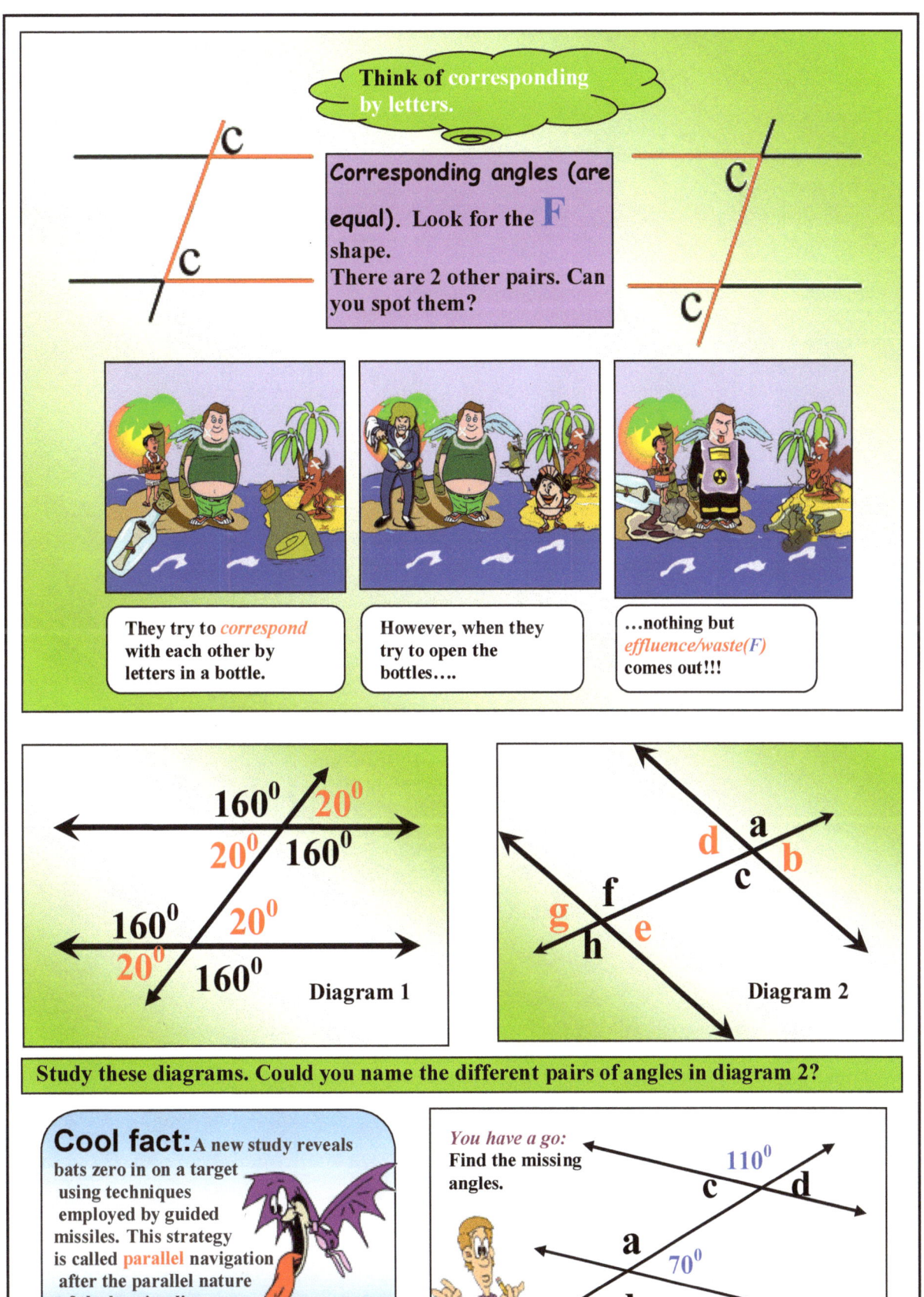

Angles in shapes and some others.

Picture an angel juggling many different shapes! A circus setting.

Remember that we will use the **angel on a stretcher** to represent 180^0 and the **rebellious angel** to represent 360^0.

Angles in a triangle add up to 180^0

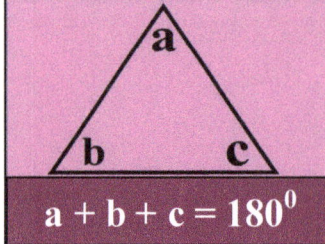

$a + b + c = 180^0$

The triangle comes to life and removes the angel on a stretcher (180^0) from his pocket. Magic trick!

Angles in a quadrilateral add up to 360^0

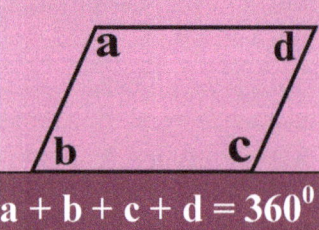

$a + b + c + d = 360^0$

The rebellious angel (360^0) rides in on a quad bike. He knocks the triangle to one side.

Angles on a straight line add up to 180^0

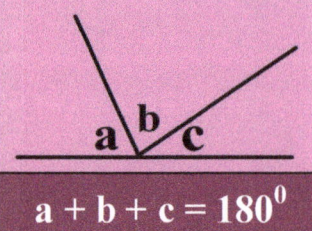

$a + b + c = 180^0$

Above him we see the angels carrying a stretcher (180^0) doing a high wire act on a straight line.

Angles around a point add up to 360^0

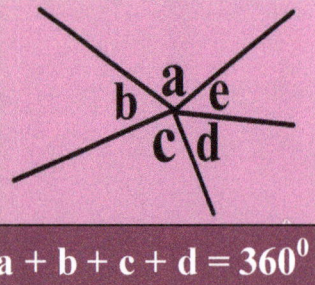

$a + b + c + d = 360^0$

An angel flies down and shoots the rebellious angel (360^0). He hits the point on target.

Cool Fact
When the Moon and the Sun are at right angles to each other and their gravitational pull partially cancels each other out, small neap tides arise.

You have a go: Find the missing angles.

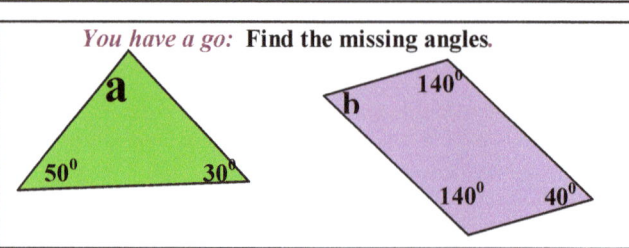

Shapes

Sounds like she-ape. So we will use this beautiful ape!

A **square** has all its sides the same length and all the angles are right angles.
4 lines of symmetry
Rotational symmetry order **4**

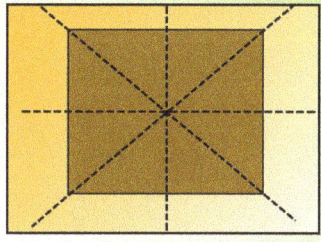

Once upon a time there lived a little pig in a **square house**. Along came a she ape who was very jealous of pig!

A **rhombus** is really a *square tilted to one side*. The only difference between the two is that the **angles are not 90⁰** in a rhombus.
2 lines of symmetry
Rotational symmetry order **2**

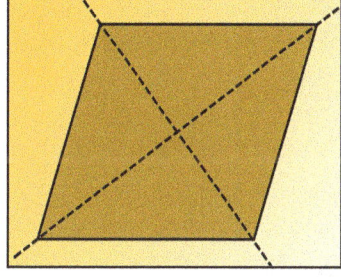

So she huffed and she puffed until she **blew the house to one side.**

A **rectangle** is a shape with 2 pairs of opposite sides that are equal and the angles are 90⁰.
2 lines of symmetry
Order of Rotational symmetry **2**

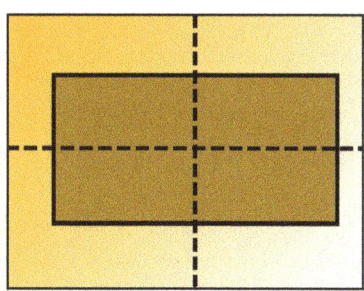

Pig then built a **rectangular house**. It should be stronger!

A **parallelogram** is really a *rectangle tilted to one side.*
No lines of symmetry
Rotational symmetry order **2**

However she ape would not be discouraged and she simply **blew this house to one side as well!**

Some other shapes that you should know:

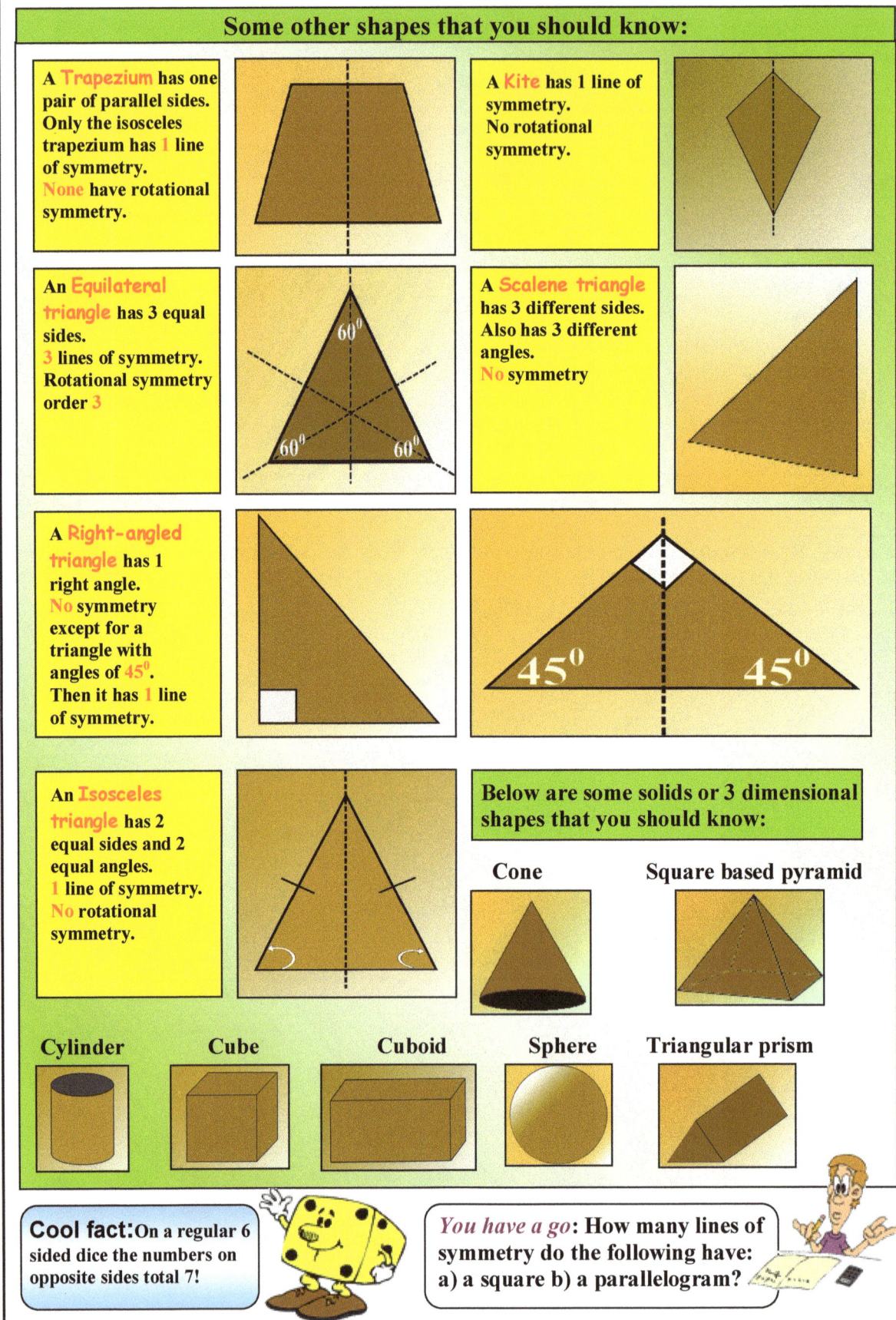

A **Trapezium** has one pair of parallel sides. Only the isosceles trapezium has **1** line of symmetry.
None have rotational symmetry.

A **Kite** has 1 line of symmetry.
No rotational symmetry.

An **Equilateral triangle** has 3 equal sides.
3 lines of symmetry.
Rotational symmetry order **3**

A **Scalene triangle** has 3 different sides. Also has 3 different angles.
No symmetry

A **Right-angled triangle** has 1 right angle.
No symmetry except for a triangle with angles of **45°**. Then it has **1** line of symmetry.

An **Isosceles triangle** has 2 equal sides and 2 equal angles.
1 line of symmetry.
No rotational symmetry.

Below are some solids or 3 dimensional shapes that you should know:

Cone   Square based pyramid

Cylinder   Cube   Cuboid   Sphere   Triangular prism

Cool fact: On a regular 6 sided dice the numbers on opposite sides total 7!

You have a go: How many lines of symmetry do the following have:
a) a square b) a parallelogram?

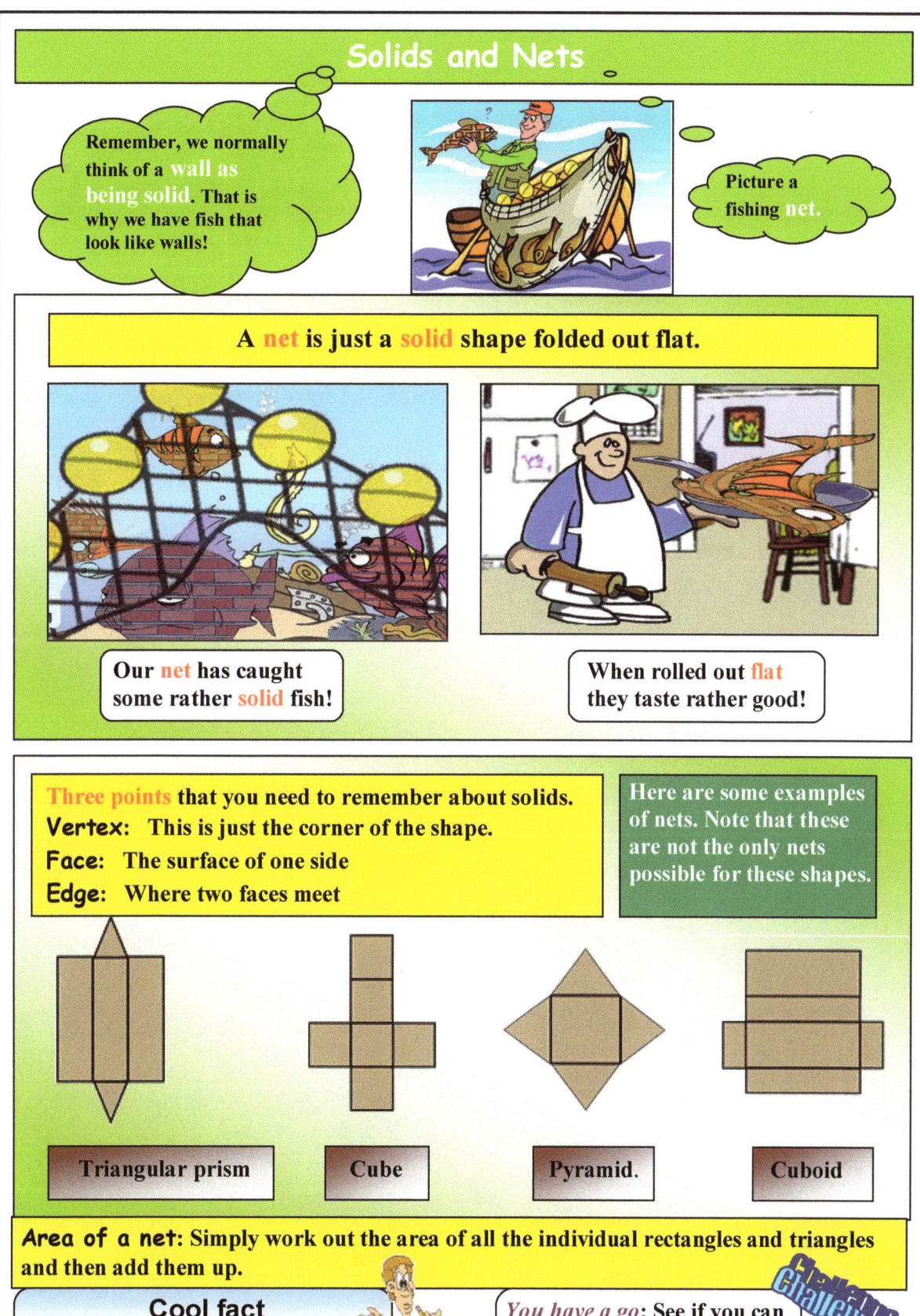

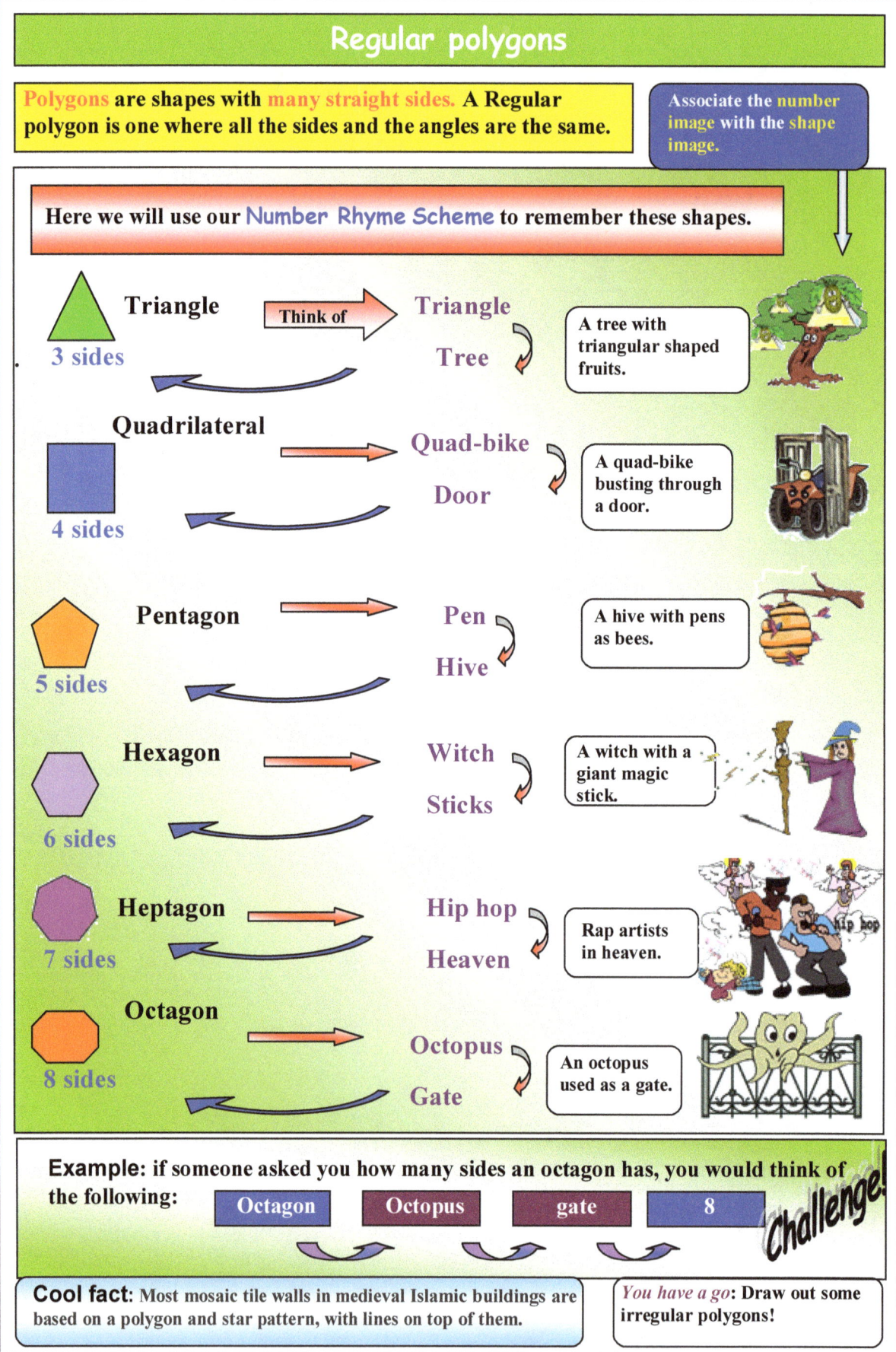

Regular Polygons

"Polly the parrot wants a cracker."

Interior and Exterior angles

Interior means **inside** and **exterior** means **outside**.

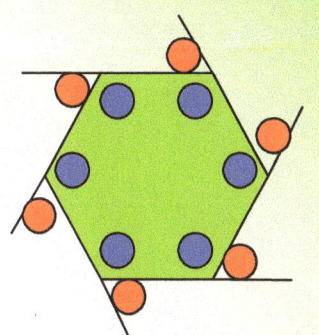

Remember that the **interior** and **exterior** angles form a straight line so they **add up to** $180°$.

You always find the **exterior** angle first.

Remember: $180°$ = angel on a stretcher.
$360°$ = rebellious angel.

$$\text{Exterior angle} = \frac{360°}{\text{No. of sides}}$$

Interior angle $= 180°$ – exterior angle

The **rebellious angel** tries to free polygon. He wants to get him **outside** by breaking the **sides** of the cage!

However he hurts polygon and he too is carried away **straight on a stretcher**! He will see the **inside** of a hospital!

Sum of the exterior angles of any polygon = $360°$

Example: Calculate the exterior and interior angles in the following shape:

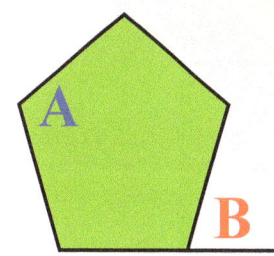

Pentagon = 5 sides
Exterior angle (B) = $360°/5 = 72°$.
Interior angle (A) = $180°$ – exterior angle
$= 180° - 72° = 108°$

Sum of the interior angles = interior angle x no. of angles

Example: find the sum of the interior angles of a regular pentagon.
Interior angle = $108°$ (from above) x 5
$= 540°$

Cool fact: Basketball players instinctively judge the correct angle of their shot to get the correct arch and resulting drop for their shot.

You have a go: Find the exterior and interior angles of a regular hexagon.

Area

A for apple

We will use our **Alphabet technique** here to learn the area of shapes.

Rectangle	**R** for ark (Sounds like ark.)	A = length x width
Triangle	**T** for tea pot	A = ½ base x height = (base x height)/2
Square	**S** for Eskimo	A = side x side
Circle	**C** for sea	A = Π x radius² (Π = pie)
Parallelogram	**P** for pea	A = base x height
Trapezium	**T** for tea pot	A = ½ (a+b) x h = ((a+b) x h)/2

Some other characters we will use : **Base = bee   height = h bomb**. If any character **splits in half** in the cartoon then it means that the number **½ is involved** somewhere!

Meet some of the characters in this story

The others are a little shy!

Copyright © Sunnil Singh 2008

Our story begins with apple going for a walk in the desert.

He sees an *ark* with *rectangular sails* and two strange characters aboard. An L shaped giraffe and a hippo. with a w shaped bow!

Rectangle: **R** for Ark $A = l \times w$

Triangle: **T** for teapot $A = \frac{1}{2} \text{ base} \times \text{height}$

A *teapot* with a *triangular hat* emerges and releases a swarm of angry *bees*.

Apple produces his *H-bomb* and is ready for action.

He detonates his bomb and splits the bee *in half*! He runs off but falls down a cliff.

Square: **S** for Eskimo $A = s \times s$ (cubes = square)

Apple lands on an *Eskimo*.

The Eskimo splits in two becoming *two identical Eskimos*. They stand *side by side*.

The Eskimos pull out ice *cubes* on a string and whirl these around as weapons to attack apple. Apple jumps into the sea.

Copyright © Sunnil Singh 2008

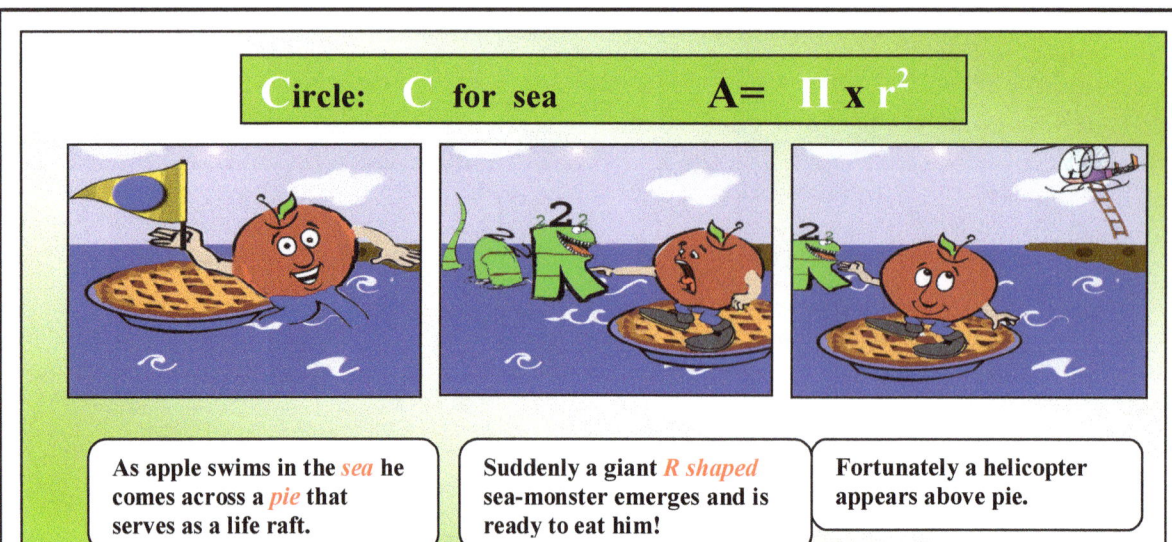
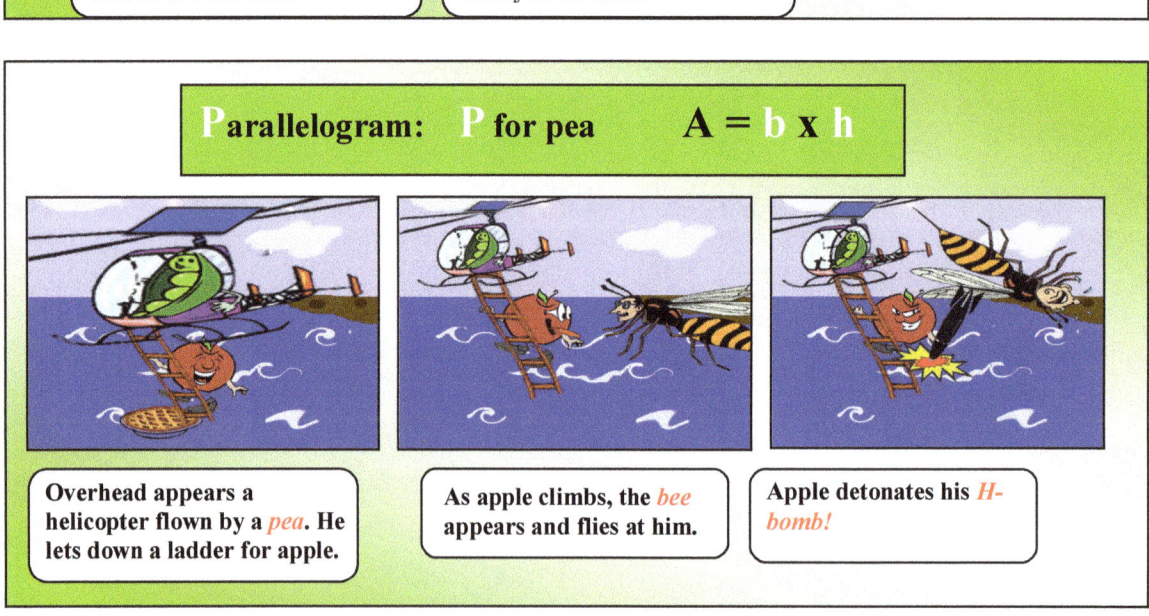

Some examples of area.

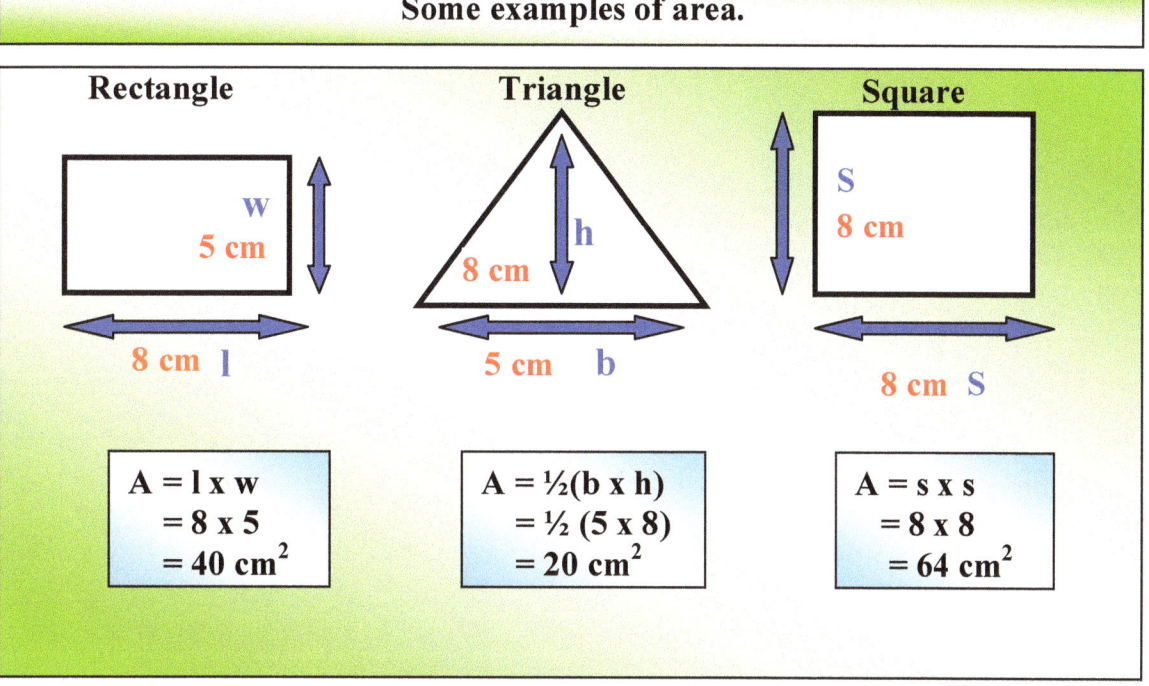

Rectangle
w = 5 cm, l = 8 cm

A = l x w
= 8 x 5
= 40 cm²

Triangle
h = 8 cm, b = 5 cm

A = ½(b x h)
= ½ (5 x 8)
= 20 cm²

Square
S = 8 cm

A = s x s
= 8 x 8
= 64 cm²

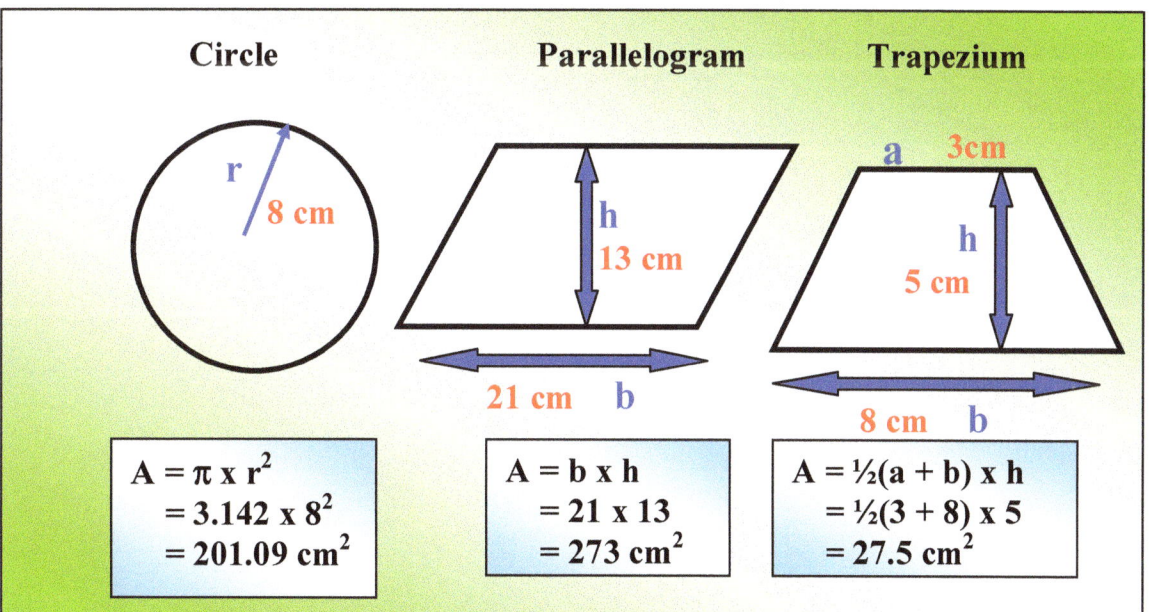

Circle
r = 8 cm

A = π x r²
= 3.142 x 8²
= 201.09 cm²

Parallelogram
h = 13 cm, b = 21 cm

A = b x h
= 21 x 13
= 273 cm²

Trapezium
a = 3 cm, h = 5 cm, b = 8 cm

A = ½(a + b) x h
= ½(3 + 8) x 5
= 27.5 cm²

Don't forget area is always *unit squared* example cm², m², mm² etc.

Cool facts
An adult human's skin typically covers 20 square feet (1.86 square metres). Only about 29% of the earth's surface area is land!

You have a go: Find the area:

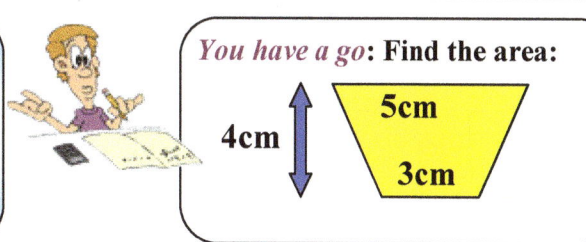

4cm, 5cm, 3cm

Copyright © Sunnil Singh 2008

Perimeter

Sounds similar to pretty-meter. So picture our pretty meter maid.

Perimeter: This is simply the distance around the outside of a shape.

Our pretty meter organises a competition where contestants try to find the distance around some shapes in rather unusual ways!

Example: find the perimeter of the following shape:

6 cm
2 cm
3 cm
6 cm
2 cm

Start at one point, adding up the lengths of the sides as you go around. Come back to where you started! Don't forget to find the missing sides as well.

Perimeter = 6cm + 3cm + 2cm + 6cm + 2cm + 6cm + 2cm + 3cm
= 30cm

Example: find the perimeter of the following shape:

2cm
5cm
5cm
2cm

Perimeter = 2cm + 5cm + 7cm + 2cm + 5cm + 3cm = 24cm

Cool Fact
Thomas Stevens was the first person to circle the globe by bicycle. The feat was accomplished between 1884 and 1886.

You have a go: Find one side of an equilateral triangle if the perimeter is $15cm^2$.

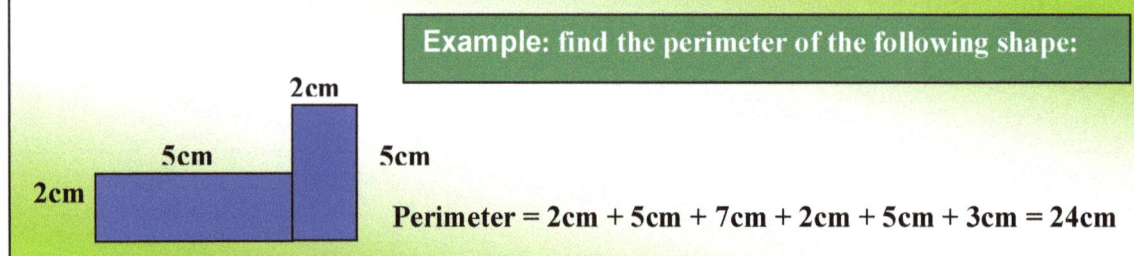

Copyright © Sunnil Singh 2008

Volume or Capacity

Volume usually makes us think of a speaker!

We see our speaker enjoying himself at a party!

Volume refers to the **amount of space** inside an object.

Remember another name for volume is **capacity**

Having drunk too much, speaker fills the bucket to **capacity**!!!
It could be that he wants to see **how much of space** is inside the bucket!

Volume of a cube = Side x Side x Side = S x S x S = S^3

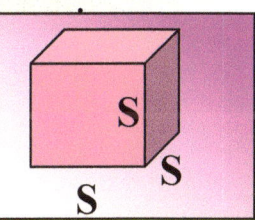

Just then a **cube** puts on a lively number while **multiplication** dances alongside the **Eskimos**.

Remember: S for Eskimo.

Volume of a Cuboid = Length x Width x Height = L x W x H

Rock star, Cuboid, shows them how its' done.
Elephant, WC and H-bomb join in.

Remember: mule stands for multiplication.
L= elephant, W= WC and H= h-bomb.

Look at the following examples.

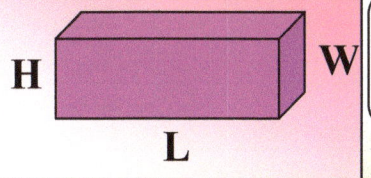

Volume = S x S x S
= 5cm x 5cm x 5cm
= $125 cm^3$

Volume = L x W x H
= 8cm x 5cm x 3c
= $120 cm^3$

Remember: the order in which you multiply does not matter, so you could have started anywhere.

Cool Fact: If Jupiter were hollow, more than one thousand Earths could fit inside.

You have a go: Find the volume of a cube with one side = 8cm.

Transformations

T for teapot.

In mathematics any movement of a shape is called a **transformation**. There are 4 types of transformations

Some crazy scientists **transform** teapot into an astronaut!

Reflections: Reflecting an object along a **mirror line** such that both sides could fold together exactly. Both shapes are said to be congruent (have the same shape and size).

Reflection in the Y axis

Reflection in the X axis

Teapot looks in a mirror to see the new him and sees his **reflections in a mirror** but also sees his future!!!

Translation: Basically movement in a **straight line**.

Shows movement in x direction
Shows movement in y direction

$\begin{pmatrix} -8 \\ 5 \end{pmatrix}$ $\begin{pmatrix} 0 \\ 6 \end{pmatrix}$

He is shot **straight** into space with his **trans**lator on board.

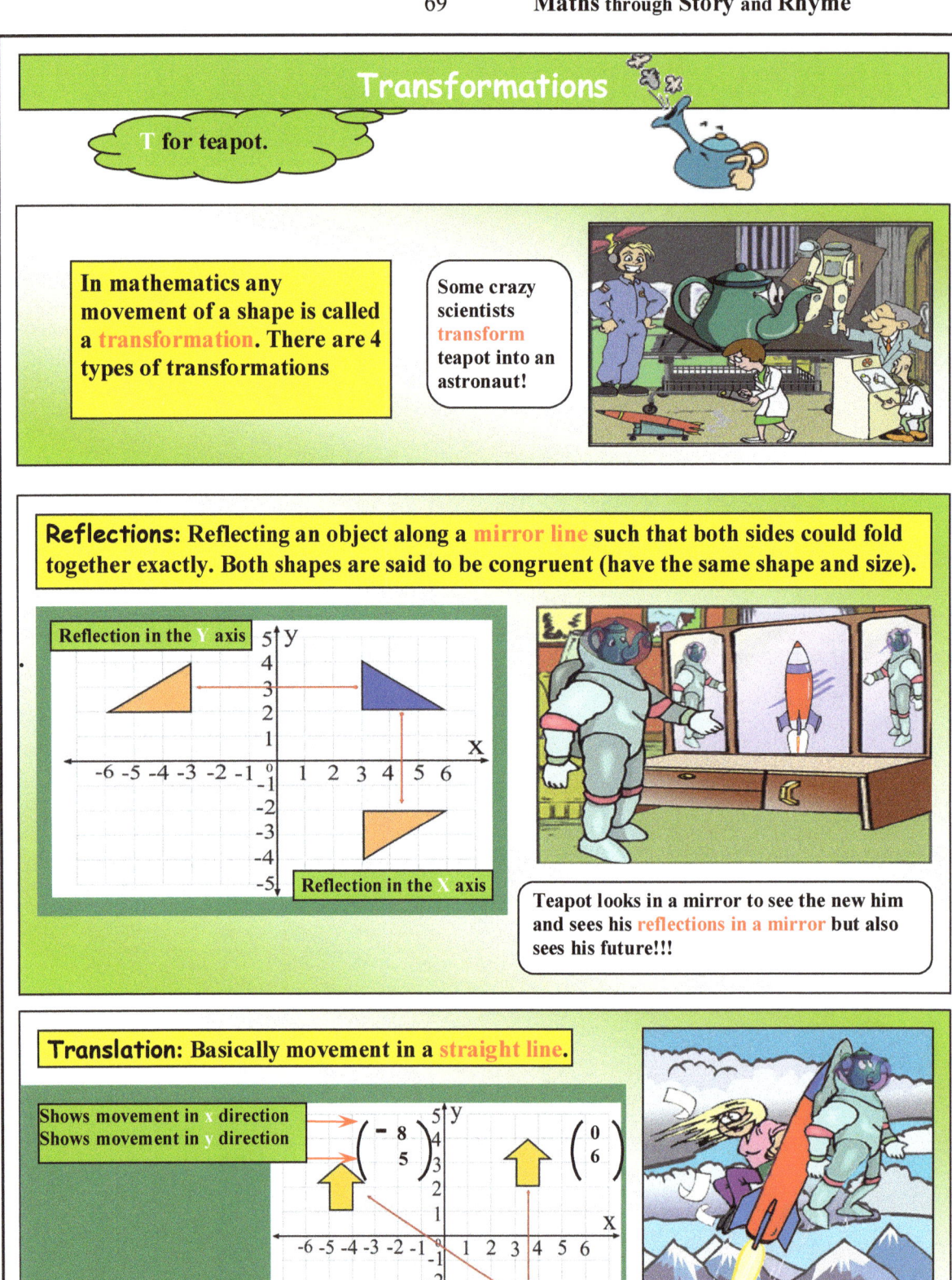

Rotations: Turns a shape through an angle about a fixed point. The fixed point is called the centre of rotation.

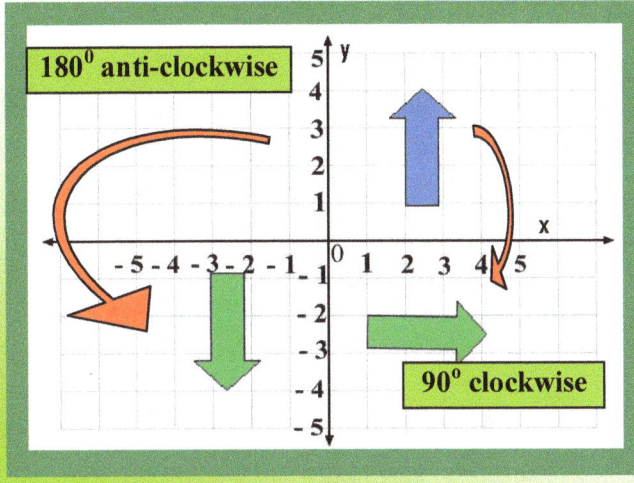

180° anti-clockwise

90° clockwise

He is then set in orbit around the earth and continues to rotate in this way.

Enlargements: Changing the size of an object. The scale factor tells us how much bigger or smaller to make the object.

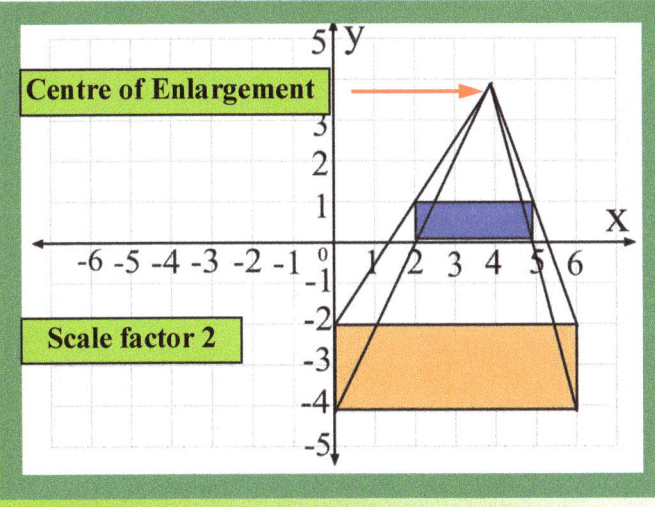

Centre of Enlargement

Scale factor 2

His trip into space has given him great power! He has been enlargened and now easily carries the earth.

Cool Facts

Metamorphosis is a biological process by which an animal physically develops and transforms from birth.

You have a go: Describe the transformation shown.

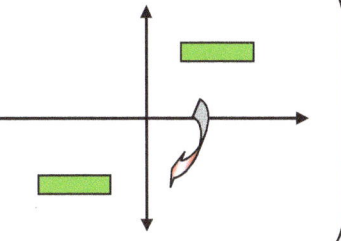

Symmetry

Sounds like: *See- my- tree*, so picture your pet tree!

Symmetry is about **changing the position** of a **picture** or **shape** but having them still **look the same**.

Now the **positions have changed** and pet tree is certainly happy!

There are 3 kinds of symmetry that you need to know:

1. Line Symmetry: this is where you have a **mirror line** dividing a shape into equal parts. You could have more than one mirror line.

Suddenly pet tree finds himself in a jungle where a giant **mirror** splits another tree **in half**!

Line Symmetry

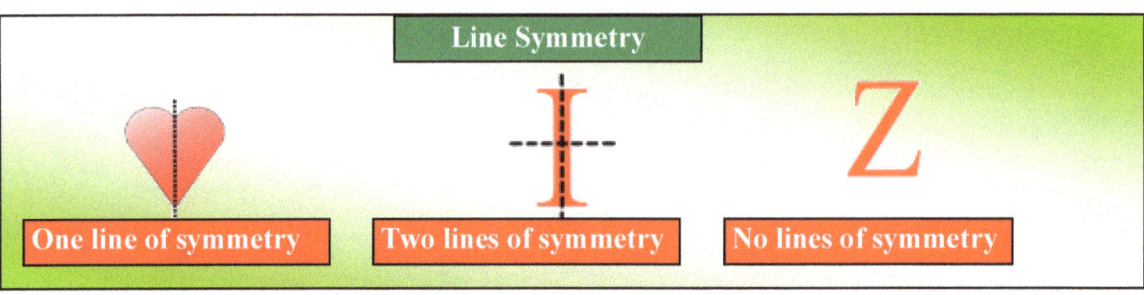

One line of symmetry | Two lines of symmetry | No lines of symmetry

How to draw reflections. Example: draw a reflection of the following

First: Reflect each point by drawing a line at 90° to the mirror line. Let each line extend to exactly the same distance on the other side.

Second: Now just join up each of the points and you have the reflected shape.

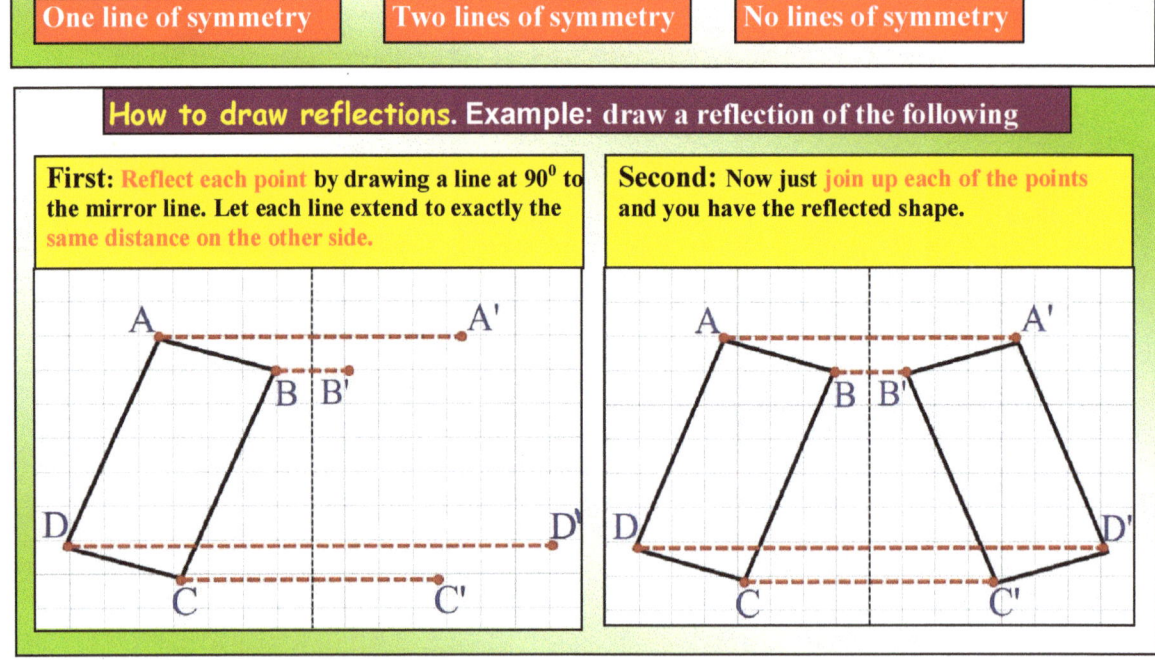

2. Plane symmetry.
Plane symmetry is found in solid 3D shapes. A shape could have many planes of symmetry.

Eager to escape, pet tree jumps onto his plane and flies off. Unfortunately he flies into a solid cloud that is built like a wall!

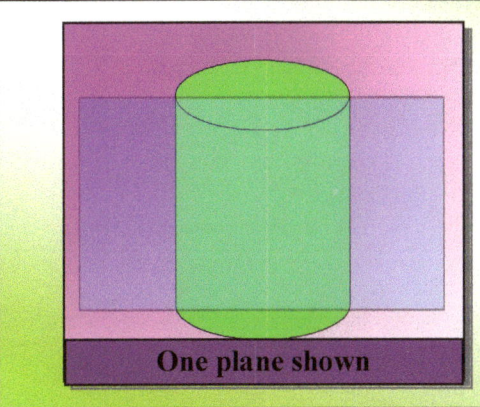

One plane shown

Two planes shown

3. Rotational Symmetry.
This is where you rotate a shape all the way around and you count the number of times that it looks exactly the same as when you started. You could say that you check how often it fits upon itself.

Fortunately pet tree escapes by using his parachute. However the parachute is a top that rotates around and around, so the accountant comes along to count how many times it rotates!

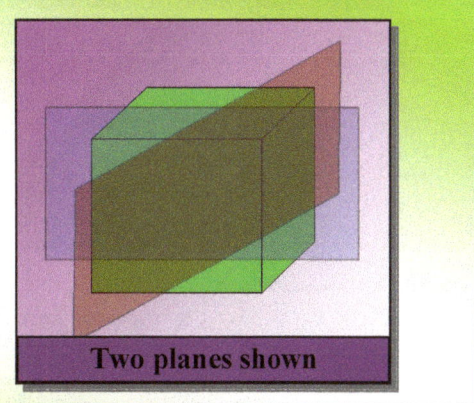

Example: What is the order of rotational symmetry for the following shape?

First pick a point on the shape.

Now count how many times the shape fits onto itself as it turns a full 360^0.

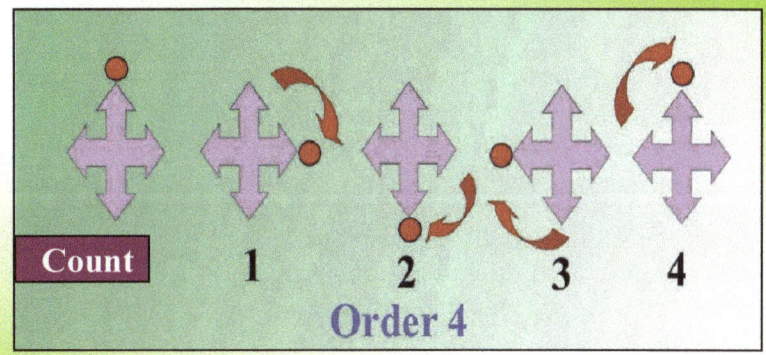

Count   1   2   3   4

Order 4

Copyright © Sunnil Singh 2008

Look at the following:

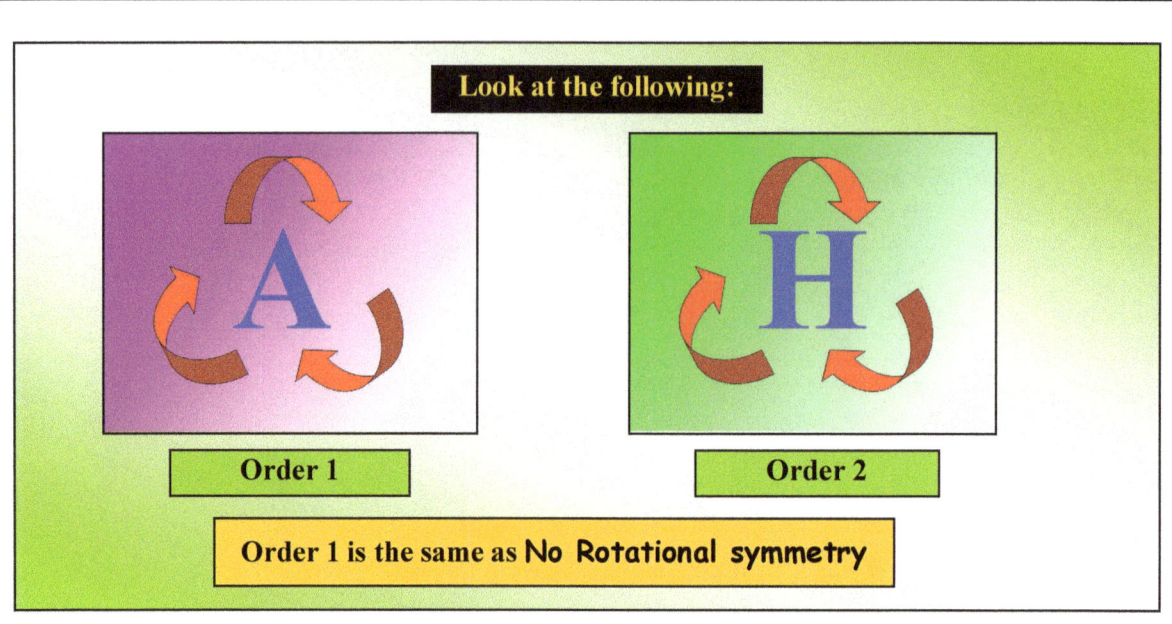

Order 1   Order 2

Order 1 is the same as No Rotational symmetry

You also need to know about tessellations.

Tessellations: This is basically a *tiling pattern with no gaps*.

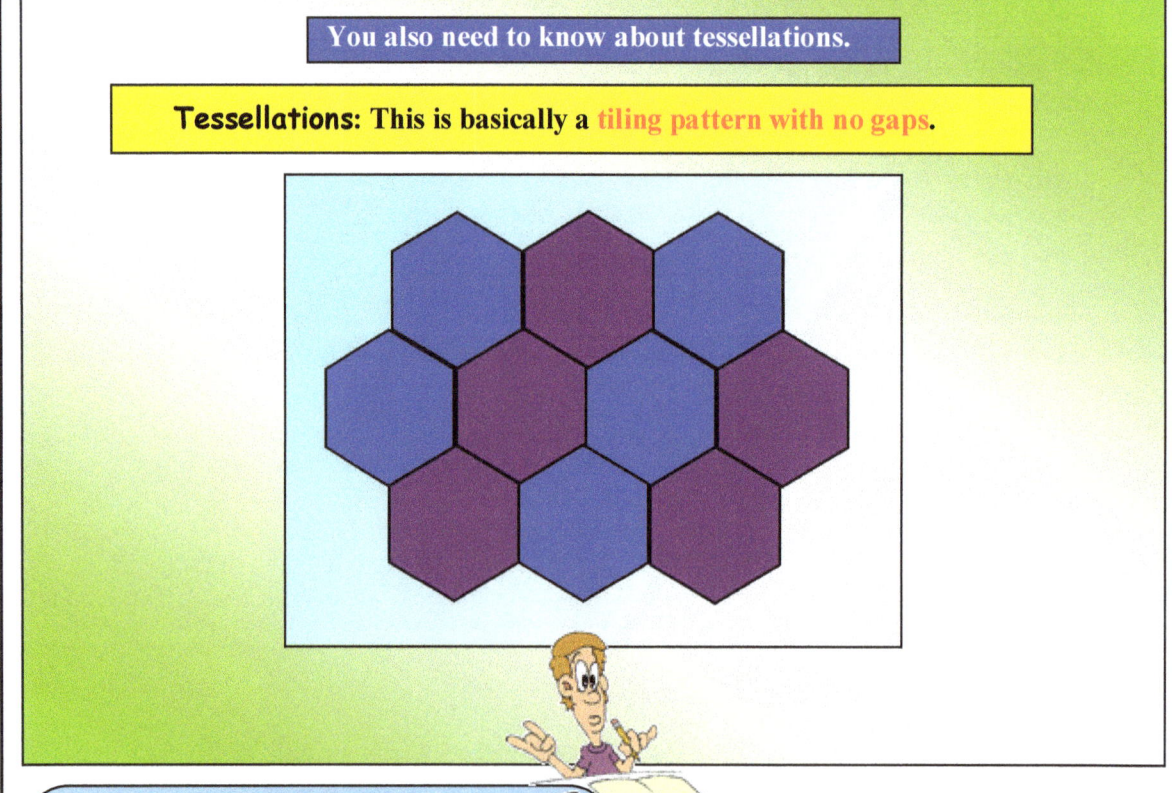

Cool Facts
Venus: the planet rotates from east to west once every 243 Earth days, in stark contrast to all other planets. Yet its orbit takes only 225 days.

You have ago: **Complete: How many**
a) lines of symmetry   b) planes of symmetry

Enlargements

Remember that enlargements are a type of transformation. So we will stick with Teapot from transformations.

Enlargement refers to **changing the size** of an object.
It can get bigger or smaller.
The shape you start with is called the **Object**.
The transformed shape is called the **Image**.
The scale factor tells us **how big or how small** to make the object.

If the **scale factor** is *bigger than 1*, then the object *gets bigger*.

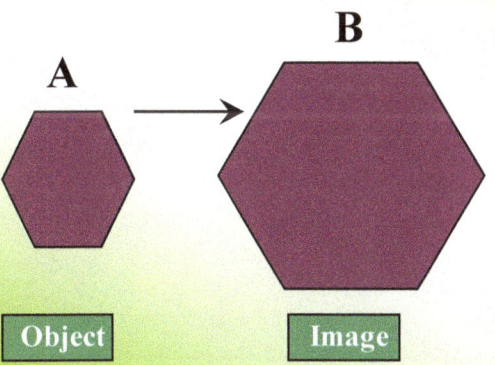

Object | Image

A to B is an enlargement using scale factor 2.

Scale uses a *big gun* to enlargen teapot.

Remember: **gun** stands for the number **one**.

If the **scale factor** is *smaller than 1*, then the object *gets smaller*.

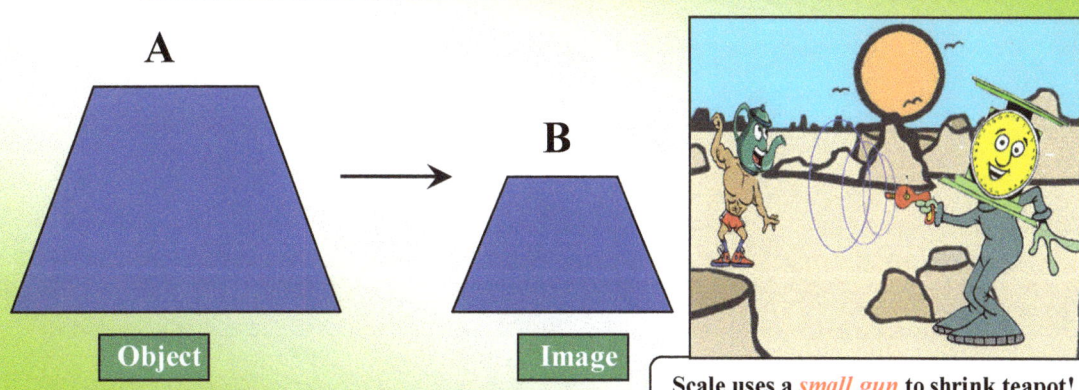

Object | Image

A to B is an enlargement using scale factor $^1/_2$.

Scale uses a *small gun* to shrink teapot!

Copyright © Sunnil Singh 2008

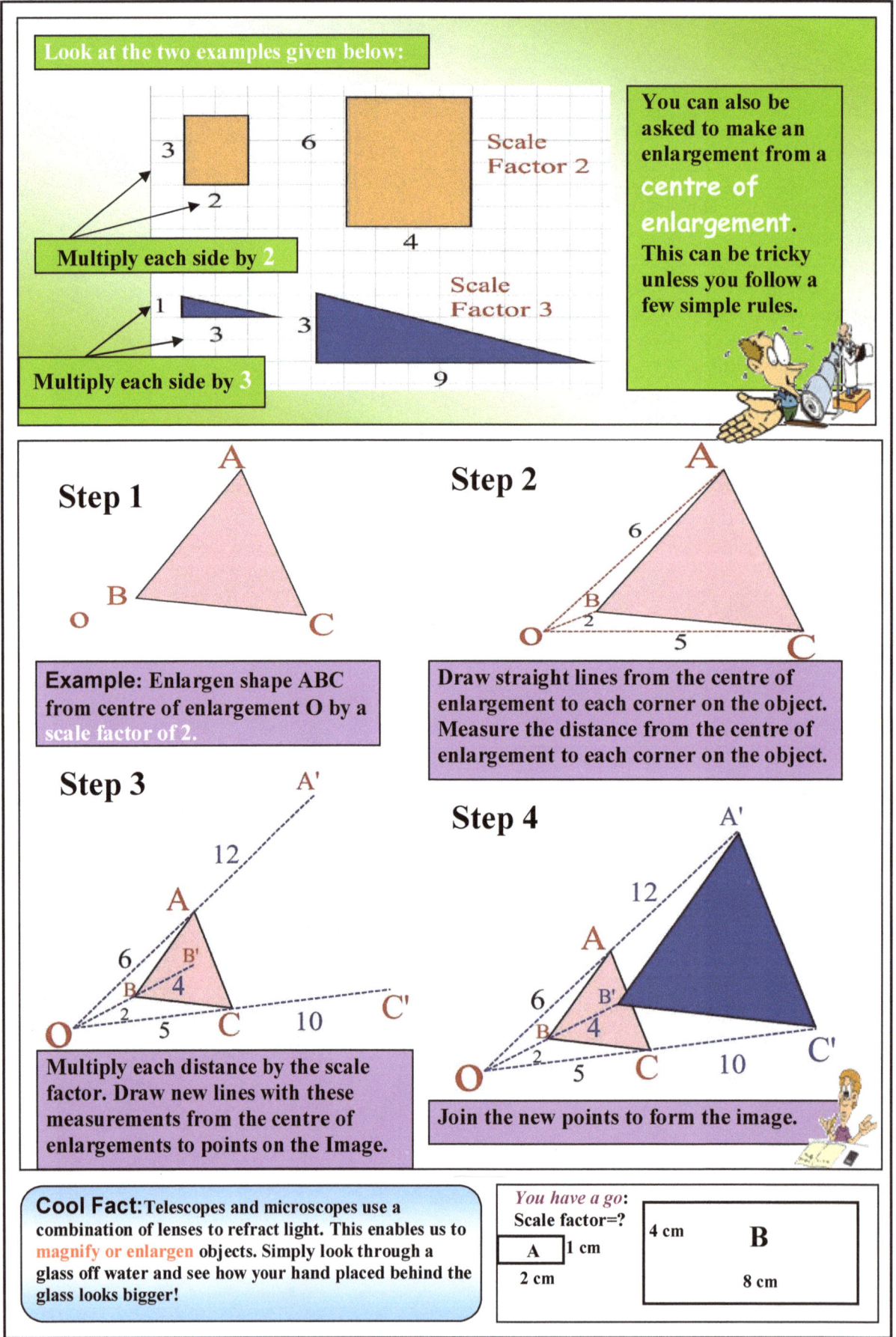

Maps

All maps must have a scale. This helps you relate the map to real life.

So map has been clever enough to find a scale!

He thinks that he has now linked the map to the real world using his scale.

Example 1: Measure the distance from point A to point C. Scale: 1cm = 50km. This means that 1cm on your map is equal to 50km in real life.

Steps to follow:

1. Place your *ruler* against the distance/s that you have to measure and *count* the number of *centimetres*.

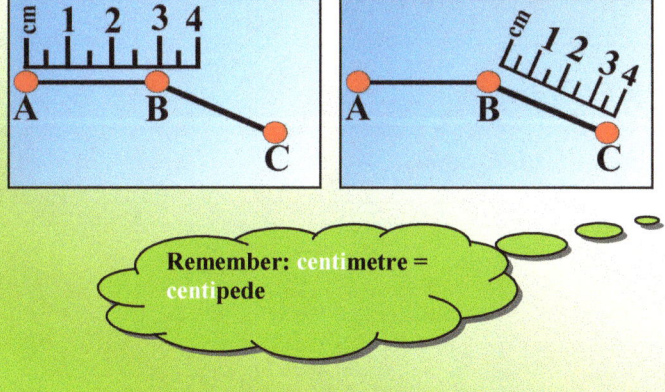

Remember: centimetre = centipede

Map tries to find the distance between his school and his home by counting the number of centipedes on his ruler.

2. *Convert* the *cm into km* using the *scale*.

Scale: 1 cm = 50 km.
So 3 cm = 150 km and
4 cm = 200 km

Remember that a long road represents kilometres.

Since centipede was in the wrong place at the wrong time, scale decides to convert him into kilometres!

3. **Add** up all the *kilometres* to get your answer.

150 km + 200 km
= 350 km

However when all the *kilometres* have been done, a race is held but *addition* is not happy about being last!

Example 2: A map is drawn on a scale of 1 cm to 2 km. If a road is 8km long in real life, how long will it be in cm on the map?

1. Draw a line that will be the road/line on the map.

_____

2. Mark off 1cm at a time and write the equivalent scale next to it.

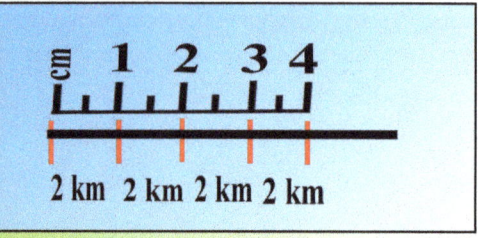

3. Stop until you get to the distance in kilometres.
2km + 2km + 2km + 2km = 8km
Now count how many cm this was on your ruler. (4cm)

You have a go:

Estimate the length of the ark shown here.
Scale: 1cm = 10m.

Cool Facts

Cartography is the art and science of making maps. The oldest known maps are preserved on Babylonian clay tablets from about 2300 B.C.

Copyright © Sunnil Singh 2008

Bearings

*Sounds like **bear-rings**, so picture a **bear wearing a ring**.*

When we express these compass directions as angles we are expressing **bearings**.

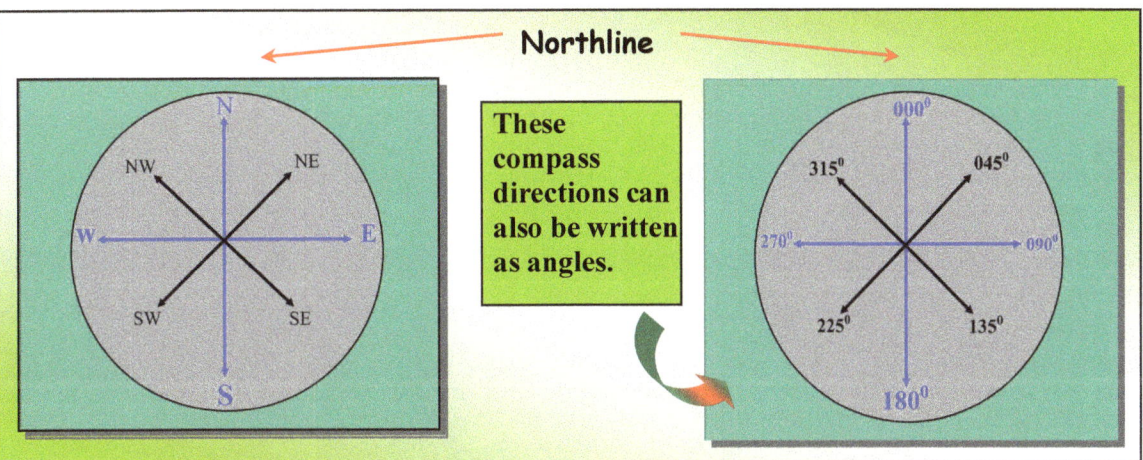

These compass directions can also be written as angles.

Some points to remember:
1. Bearings are always *measured clockwise* from the **Northline**.
2. Bearings are written as *3 figures* example, $035°$ rather than $35°$.

Follow these easy steps to **find bearings**:

| To find bearings: | Measure the bearing clockwise from the **Northline**. | Draw the **Northline** at the point from where you are looking/moving. |

Bear is lost and tries **to find** his way home.

He has to get **from the old tree** to his **home**. So he has to draw a **northline** at the old tree.

He then tries to **measure** the bearing **clockwise**.

Copyright © Sunnil Singh 2008

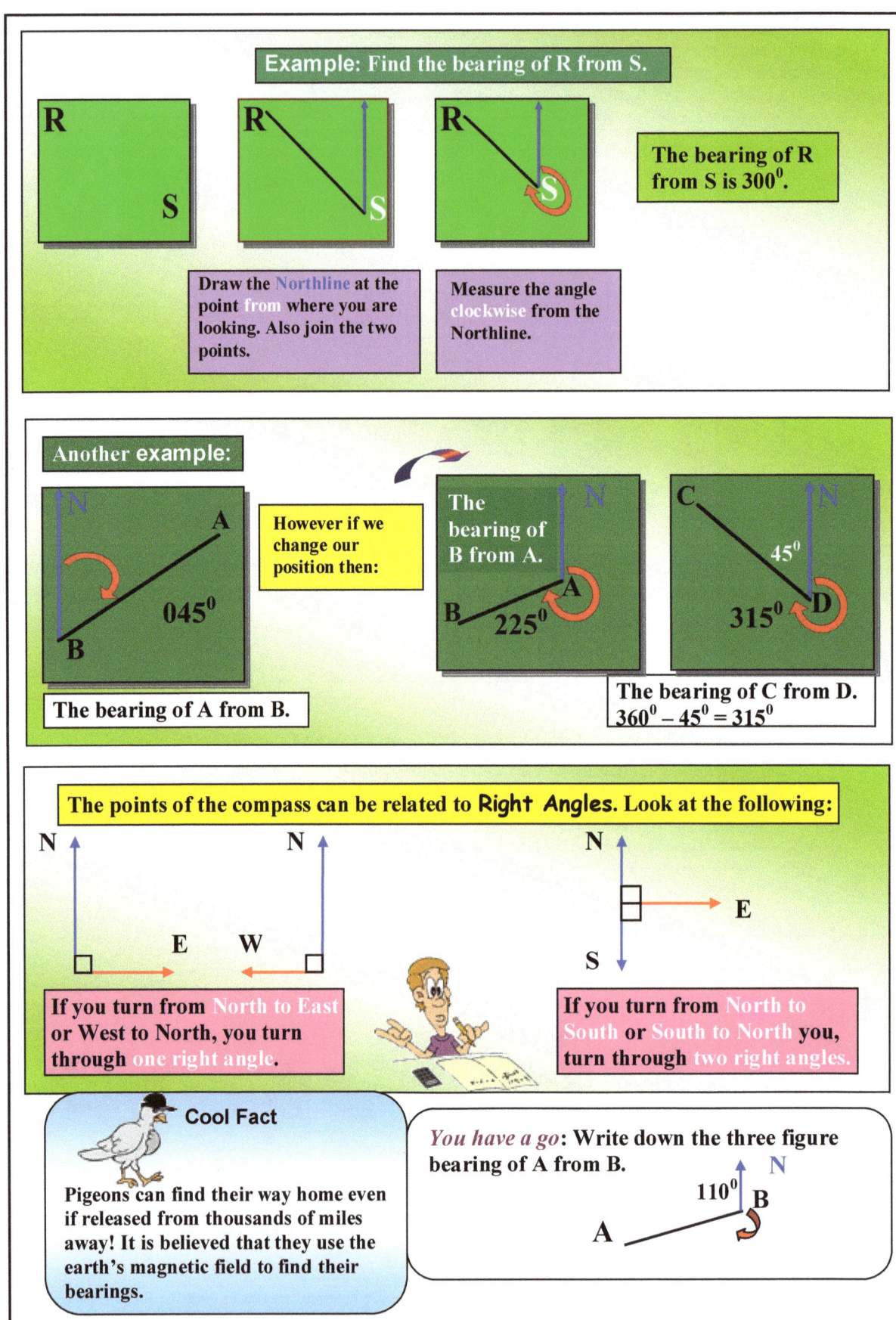

Recap and Review of Shapes

A little 'R and R' never hurt anyone!

You think!

1. Name and describe each of the 6 basic angles that you have learnt so far.
2. Complete the following:
   2.1 Angles around a point add up to _____.
   2.2 Two angles that add up to $180°$ are called _____.
   2.3 Alternate angles are _____.
   2.4 Corresponding angles are _____.
3. In each of the following diagrams find the value of the letter.

a)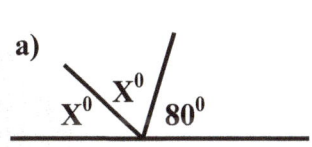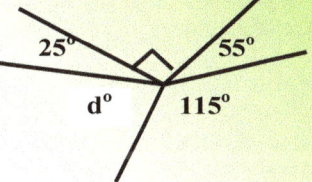

4. a) Write down the angle that corresponds to $h°$.
   b) Write down the angle that is alternate to $i°$

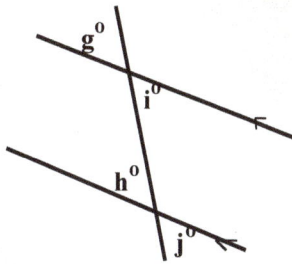

5. Describe the following transformation:

6. How many sides does a heptagon have?

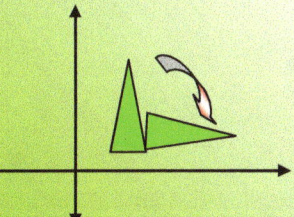

7. How does a rectangle differ from a parallelogram?
8. What is the formula for the area of a trapezium?
9. Define volume and perimeter.
10. List the 3 kinds of symmetry that you have learnt.
11. In enlargements, what does the scale factor tell us?

Algebra

Number Patterns

N for entrance

P for Pea

Pea enters a magical world guided by a genie.

Here are the basic types of number patterns that you should know.

Add or subtract the same number each time.

Pea is led through the first entrance by addition and subtraction. They find a group of aliens playing sports with the same number!

2   4   6   8   10
  +2 +2 +2 +2
Rule: add 2 each time.

20   16   12   8   4
   -4   -4   -4   -4
Rule: Subtract 4 each time.

Add or subtract a changing number.

Addition and subtraction led pea through the next entrance and discover a group of magical fairies at a party. The fairies pair of with different numbers and change partners when not happy.

3   5   8   12   17
  +2 +3 +4   +5
Rule: Add one extra number each time.

20   18   14   8   0
   -2   -4   -6   -8
Rule: Subtract two extra each time.

Copyright © Sunnil Singh 2008

Multiply or divide by the same number each time.

Multiplication and division lead Pea through the next entrance. Here they find a super hero training camp. The hero is training using the same number!

3　9　27　81
　x 3　x 3　x 3
Rule: Multiply by 3 each time.

300　30　3　0.3
　÷ 10　÷ 10　÷ 10
Rule: Divide by 10 each time

Add the previous two terms.

Since Pea has had such a long and strange journey, addition decides to serve him with a treat: two delicious termites!

Term: think of termite

1　2　3　5　8　13　21

1+1　2+1　2+3　3+5　5+8　8+13

Rule: add the previous 2 terms to get the next term.

This is a special number sequences called the Fibonacci sequence.

Look at the following when we continue the sequence:
…34　55　89　144　233… divide each number by the one before.

$55 ÷ 34 = 1.618$

$89 ÷ 55 = 1.618$ and so on … this is called the **Golden Number** or **Golden Ratio**

Cool Fact
If you divide the distance from your head to your toes by the distance from your belly button to your toes, you get the Golden Number.

You have a go: Write down the next two numbers in each sequence:

a) 6, 8, 10, 12 …　b) 10, 6, 2, -2…

Finding the nth term

*Finding the en**lightened** **term**ite!!!*

*Term so think of **term**ite.*

The nth term of a sequence is simply the rule that helps you find **any term** in the sequence.

Our enlightened term examines a sequence of numbers and finds a **term**ite hiding among them!

First Type: Where there is a common difference

Example: Find the nth term for this sequence: 5   8   11   14   17   20 …

First: find the **gap** between the numbers.

5   8   11   14   17   20 …

+3   +3   +3   +3   +3

This is called the **Common Difference**. It gives you the first part of the formula. Just multiply the Common Difference by the letter **n**. Here it will be **3n**.

Determined to get rid of the termite that is hiding between the numbers, our enlightened term forces apart the numbers and looks between the **gaps** to find the culprit. **Subtraction** offers to help.

Remember that Difference refers to subtraction.

Second: compare the original sequence with the **common difference** sequence and see what needs to **added or subtracted** to make both sequences the same.

Determined that the cleaner sequence (one with no termites) be found, the enlightened termite **compares two sequences** and declares the second sequence the winner!

Term number (n)	1	2	3	4	5	6
Original Sequence	5	8	11	14	17	20 …
	+2	+2	+2	+2	+2	+2
Value of 3n	3	6	9	12	15	18

(n stands for term number)

We still need to **add 2**. Now put both together.

So the **nth term** or formula will be ➔ **3n + 2**

Copyright © Sunnil Singh 2008

Let's test it: Say I wanted the 4th term: (we know it should be 14)

n^{th} term $= 3n + 2$

(4th term so n = 4) $= 3 \times 4 + 2 = 14$ so **it works!!!**

So if someone asked you to find say the 30th term you would do the following:

n^{th} term $= 3n + 2$

(30th term so n = 30) $= 3 \times 30 + 2 = 92$

Second Type: Where there is no common difference at first.

Example: Find a formula for the nth term of the number sequence:
5, 19, 41, 71, 109…

First: Look for a difference (gap) between the terms:

5   19   41   71   109
+14 +22 +30 +38   no common difference
  +8   +8   +8   now look at the **second difference**

Second: Since there is a common difference here the first part of the formula must contain n^2

Now divide the common difference by 2 and then multiply by n^2. ($^8/_2 = 4$)

So the first part of the formula will be $4n^2$

Third: Now compare the original sequence with the n^2

Term number (n)	1	2	3	4	5
Sequence	5	19	41	71	109
	+1	+3	+5	+7	+9
Value of $4n^2$	4	16	36	64	100

Fourth: Now find a formula for this part as before:

Term number (n)	1	2	3	4	5
Sequence	1	3	5	7	9

+2 +2 +2 +2   but also −1

Value of 2n   2   4   6   8   10

So the second part of the formula will be $2n - 1$ Formula for n^{th} term will be:

$$4n^2 + 2n - 1$$

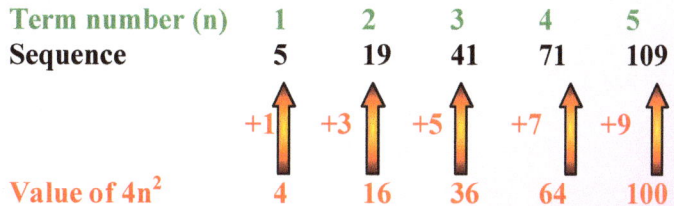

Cool Fact: The continents from largest to smallest are: Asia, Africa, North America, South America, Antarctica, Europe and Australia.

You have a go: Find the first 5 terms of a sequence that has an nth term of $4n-1$.

Special Number Sequences

Here are some of the special number sequences that you need to know:

Even numbers: 2 4 6 8 10 12 14… this is your 2 times table
They always end in 0, 2, 4, 6 or 8.

Odd numbers: 1 3 5 7 9 11 13…
They always end in 1, 3, 5, 7 or 9.

Hint: even numbers divide by 2 but odd numbers don't

Square numbers:
1 4 9 16 25 36 49…
They are called Square numbers since they form the areas of squares.

Think of squares on a chessboard.

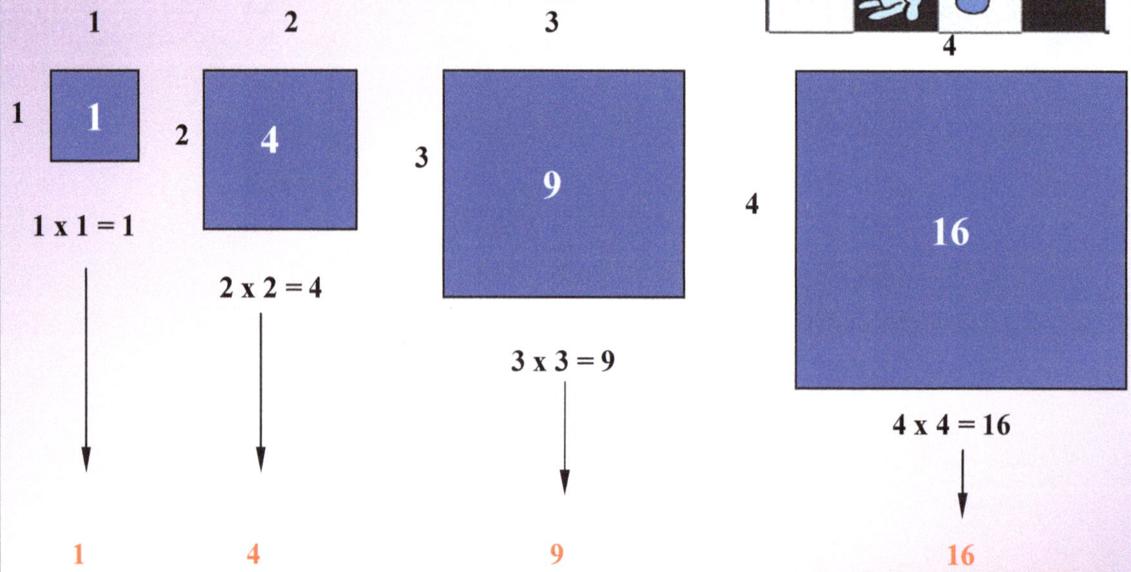

1   2   3   4

1 × 1 = 1

2 × 2 = 4

3 × 3 = 9

4 × 4 = 16

1   4   9   16

So you can easily form a square number from any number by just multiplying the number by itself. Example: use 3, (3 × 3 = 9, which is therefore a square number).

Multiplication oversees a game of chess between 3 and 3, but they are not playing by the rules. They push chess pieces off the table!

He calls in 9 to help but 9 is even worse as he makes the chess pieces fight each other! Multiplication is really mad.

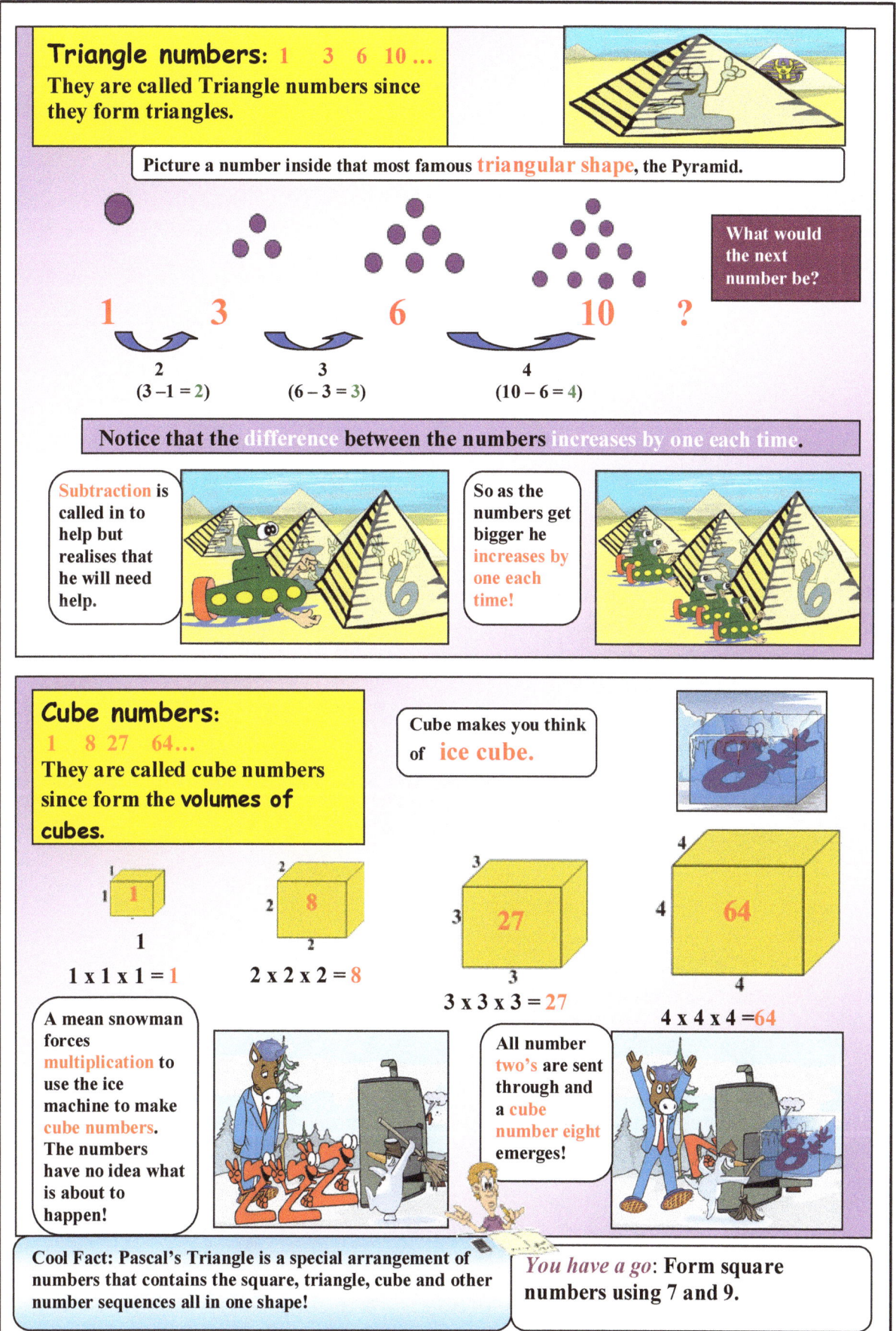

Square Roots

Refer to the section on squaring of a number since **square roots** are the **opposite** of finding the **square of a number.**

*Square roots so think of a **tree** with its **roots** coming out of the **squares on a chessboard!***

Square root of a number is the opposite of finding the square of a number.

Nine used to play with the chess pieces, but now the **opposite happens**. The chess pieces get to play with the numbers!

Frightened, nine goes back to his roots of being a three hoping that they go easy on him!

Example:

Squaring
$3^2 = 3 \times 3 = 9$
Square root

So the **Square root** of a number is that number which when multiplied by itself gives the original number.

Example: $\sqrt{9} = 3$ (since $3 \times 3 = 9$)
$\sqrt{16} = 4$ (since $4 \times 4 = 16$)
$\sqrt{25} = 5$ (since $5 \times 5 = 25$) and so on…

$\sqrt{}$
We use this special symbol for square roots.

Cool Fact
You can use square roots to find the distance to the horizon when standing on the beach. It depends on the height of your eyes above the water. You can use the formula, $d = \sqrt{13h}$, where h is the height in metres of your eyes.

You have a go:
Find the square roots of the following numbers:
a) $\sqrt{64}$ b) $\sqrt{81}$ c) $\sqrt{100}$

Collecting like terms

*Think of bus **term**inal or **term**ite.*

Simplifying or **collecting** like terms means putting together terms that have **exactly the same letters**.

The termite bus conductor wants to **collect** the **like** termites together.

The termites with the **same letters** get together. Those without letters are on their own.

Example: Simplify $2x + 5y + 8x + 4 - 4y + 1 + 8y - x$

First find all the terms that are the same. Put **shapes** around terms to help you.

Second: just put all the same terms together. Remember to include the sign of the term.

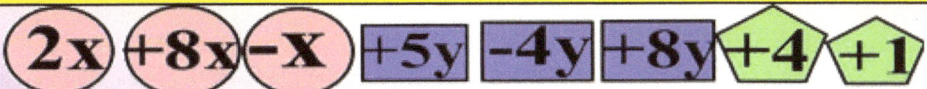

Third: **combine** the **like terms** and remember to use the **number line** to help you.

Answer = $9x + 9y + 5$

Cool Facts
Waiters in restaurants often use a form of algebra when taking orders. They use letters to represent items on the menu. So $1Bs + 2Lc + 3C$, might mean:
1 beef **s**tew + **2 l**amb **c**urries + **3 c**okes.

You have a go: **Simplify:**
$4a^2 + 14a^2 - 23b + 3b^3$

B and b^3 are not like terms. Like terms must have the same power.

Balancing: An introduction to equations.

Equations make us think of *equal to*.
So picture our 'equal to' character.

Have you seen this before?
x + 5 = 12   or this 2y + 3 = 11

All they require is to find the special number that makes the

left hand side = right hand side!

We have to *balance* the two sides.

Equal has a twin. Are things balanced now?

```
    x + 5   =   12
Left hand side   Right hand side
      x = 7  (since 7+5=12)
```

Cool Fact
The longest recorded duration for balancing on one foot is 76 hr 40 min by Arulanantham Suresh Joachim (Sri Lanka), from May 22-25, 1997.

a) x − 8 = 20
    x = 28 (since 28−8 = 20)
b) $^{12}/a = 4$
    a = 3 (since $^{12}/3 = 4$)
c) d x 6 = 30
    d = 5 (since 5 x 6 = 30)

Multiplying out brackets

Sounds like *racket*.
So picture a tennis racket.

When multiplying out brackets the number or letter *outside* the bracket is *multiplied* by each term *inside* the bracket.

One tennis player is *outside* while the other is *inside*. How crazy!

Hint

Example: 9 (8x + 7)
=   72x   + 63

Example: 5a (3b − 2c)
=   15 ab − 10 ac

When multiplying letters just write them next to each other:
r x s = rs

Example: 5 (5y + 8x − 9)
=   25 y + 40x − 45

Example: 2r (3s − 5t + 8r)
=   6rs − 10rt + 16r^2

You have a go: multiply out:
a) 2a(4b − 5c)   b) 6x(2x − 4y)

Making formulas using words

Remember words are powerful. We can cast mathemagical spells!

Some of our spells!

The trick to creating a formula is to understand what the words mean. This is usually figuring out what operation they are referring to.

Addition	Subtraction	Multiplication	Division
Increase	Difference between	Multiplied by	Share
More	Decrease	Product	Divisible by
Plus	Take from	Times table	Divide
Total	Take away	Times	Group
Add	Minus	Lots of	Divide into
Sum	Fewer	Groups of	Share equally
And	Reduce	Multiply	Divided by
Together	Subtract		

Let's start easy:

Example: Write a formula to show the value of y when x is multiplied by 2 and we then subtract 5.

Since we are looking for y, this goes on the LHS (left hand side), so we get:

y =   x is multiplied by 2 (2x)   then   subtract 5 (-5). Now put all this together:

$$y = 2x - 5$$

More difficult example:

Example: Write a formula to show that the amount of money M that each of 3 friends gets when £100 is shared equally.

Remember shared means division. Since we are looking for M, it goes onto the left hand side of the equation. $M = 100/3$

Example: What does it cost, T, to fill a tank of petrol at 90p per litre (L)?

Remember per means multiplication. T will go on the left hand side since that is what we are looking for. $T = 90 \times L$

Cool Fact: Albert Einstein developed the formula (called: mass-energy equivalence formula).
$E = mc^2$ [Energy = Mass x (speed of light)^2]. This formula was used in the development of the atomic bomb.

You have a go: Paul thinks of a number(n). He doubles the number and then adds three. Write down an expression for Paul's answer.

Copyright © Sunnil Singh 2008

Powers

Picture a superhero.

Our super hero has a power ball of numbers! Just like the power or indices of numbers.

Powers or indices is a short way of writing out a rather long multiplication! Just that we have the **same number being multiplied by itself**.

He is confronted by a monster and so gets his *power* of 3 ready!

The same hero is now *multiplied* 3 times (*by itself*) and is ready to fight!

---

6 to the **power** 4 is written as
6^4
This simply means:
$6^4 = 6 \times 6 \times 6 \times 6$

power
6^4
Base

$3^2 = 3 \times 3 = 9$
(3 **squared** = 9)

$5^3 = 5 \times 5 \times 5 = 125$
(5 **cubed** = 125)

Anything to the **power** **1** remains the same.

$5^1 = 5$ $125^1 = 125$

Anything to the **power 0 = 1** !!!

$6^0 = 1$ $256^0 = 1$

Note: fractional indices.
$9^{1/2} = \sqrt{9} = 3$
$125^{1/3} = \sqrt[3]{125} = 5$

Cool Facts

10^{10} is called ten billion. A Googol is 10^{100}. The number of cells in the human body (more than 10^{14}).

You have a go: Find the following:

a) 12^2 b) 9^3 c) $100^{1/2}$

°F and °C Temperature Formulas

Since **temperature** normally makes us think of heat, picture these two **flaming heroes**.

Degrees Fahrenheit (°F)   **Degrees Celsius (°C)**

It is useful to have an idea about these temperature formulas:

Meanwhile our heroes prepare for battle.

$$F = \tfrac{9}{5} C + 32 \quad \text{and} \quad C = \tfrac{5}{9}(F - 32)$$

Remember: Line = 9 and hive = 5. $\tfrac{9}{5}$ shown by hive hanging low and $\tfrac{5}{9}$ shown by hive being higher up.

Fahrenheit gets addition to ride the chariot. **Addition** has his **line** and bee **hive** ready for battle. Horse **32** stands by.

Celsius gets **subtraction** to ride his chariot. His **hive is higher up** and he also has a horse **32**.

Remember these **patterns**. The 9 and the 5 are reversed in each formula. Addition and then subtraction (it's opposite) are used.

Example:
Convert a temperature of 100°C into °F. First write the formula and then substitute.
$F = \tfrac{9}{5} C + 32$
$F = \tfrac{9}{5} \times 100 + 32$
$F = 212\ °F$
Note: **100°C** or **212°F** is the **boiling point of water.**

Example:
Convert 32 °F into °C. Again just rewrite the formula and then substitute the value given.
$C = \tfrac{5}{9}(F - 32)$
$C = \tfrac{5}{9}(32 - 32)$
$C = \tfrac{5}{9} \times 0$
$C = 0\ °C$
Note: **0 °C** is the **freezing point of water.**

Our heroes are at *boiling point* with each other! Celsius has told him a *100* times to back off!

From heroes to *zeros* as their fires are *frozen* when extinguisher cools things off!

Cool Facts
The normal temperature for a human is about 37 °C (98.6 °F).
The coldest place on Earth is the South Pole or the Antarctica.

You have a go:
Convert 60 °F into °C.

Copyright © Sunnil Singh 2008

Trial and improvement

"Trial, so think of a court setting."

Goldie locks is the Judge and she is about to send the bears to jail!

In the meanwhile baby bear is trying to balance the scales of justice!

Solving equations simply means finding the value of the letter, usually x, which makes the equation true.
the left hand side = right hand side.

Equations, therefore we cannot forget our equal character.

To **solve equations** we will **substitute** different numbers for x until we find one that works.

With the bears sent off to jail, Goldie Locks runs off to their home to take their place! Will she be their *substitute*?

Example: Solve the equation:
$5x + 89 = 144$ Lets' try $x = 9$
$5 \times 9 + 89 = 144$
$45 + 89 = 144$
$134 = 144$

LHS ≠ RHS (Answer is too small so try a bigger number for x).

Mother bear's chair is too small and Goldie Locks is mad. She needs a bigger chair.

Try a bigger number, $x = 13$
$5x + 89 = 144$
$5 \times 13 + 89 = 144$
$65 + 89 = 144$
$154 = 144$

LHS ≠ RHS (Answer is too big so try a smaller number for x).

Father bear's chair is too big and Goldie Locks falls off. She needs something a bit smaller!

Try a number between 9 and 13, $x = 11$
$5x + 89 = 144$
$5 \times 11 + 89 = 144$
$55 + 89 = 144$
$144 = 144$

LHS = RHS (Answer is just right ! so $x = 11$)

Baby bear's chair is just right!!!

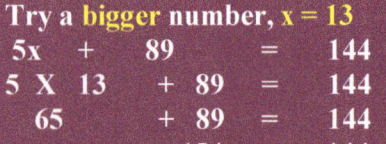

Cool Fact
The International Court of Justice (known colloquially as the World Court or ICJ) is the primary judicial organ of the United Nations.

You have a go: Solve the following equation:
$2x + 12 = 100$

Recap and Review of Algebra

1. 1.1 List the number patterns that you have learnt in this section.
    1.2 Write down the next two numbers in each sequence:
    a) 6, 8, 10, 12 …   b) 10, 6, 2, -2…
    1.3 Write down a rule for continuing each sequence:
    a) 1, 4, 7, 10…   b) 100, 10, 1, 0.1…

2. n^{th} term
    2.1 What do we mean by the nth term of a sequence?
    2.2 Describe how you would find the nth term when there is a common difference?
    2.3 Describe how you would find the nth term when there is no common difference?
    2.4 Look at the following:

    Pattern 1   Pattern 2   Pattern 3

    Draw a table showing the Patten number and the Number of squares.

    Find a rule (the nth term) for the number of squares in terms of the pattern number.

3. Special number Sequences
    3.1 What do even numbers end in?
    3.2 What do odd numbers end in?
    3.3 Give a short sequence of: a) square numbers b) cube numbers.
    3.4 Define a square root and give an example.

4. Collecting terms
    4.1 Simplify the following by collecting like terms:
    a) $2 + 3x - x$ b) $7y + y + 13 - 8$ c) $5a + 8 - 2a + 2$ easy
    4.2 Simplify:
    a) $2xy - 4 + 5yx$ b) $6t - 3y + t + 8y - 2$ c) $2a^2 - 6b + a^2 - 5b^2$ harder

5. Equations
    5.1 What must we always try to do with the two sides of an equation?
    5.2 Solve the equation $x - 6 = 16$.

6. Simplify the following: $12y(3x - 6)$.

7. Forming equations
    a) Paul thinks of a number. He doubles the number and then adds three. Write down an expression for Paul's answer. Easy
    b) Michael thinks of a number. He multiplies it by 5 and then subtracts 8. The answer is 27. What is the number? Harder

8. Powers
    8.1 Why do we use powers?
    8.2 What is the value of: a) 6^3 b) $216^{1/3}$

9. Convert 200 ^{0}C into ^{0}F.

10. Trial and Improvement
    Use trial and improvement to solve the following equation:
    a) $5b - 9 = 6$ Easy
    b) $15 = 4 + 11x$ Harder

Copyright © Sunnil Singh 2008

Data

Representing Data

> Data often makes you think of a *data disk* or *cd*.

There are a variety of ways that you could use to represent data. Know the ones listed below.

Our story begins:

Data disk has had a really trying day at the office.

Bar Charts: These use *bars* to represent information. The *height* of the bar tells us the number of items that are represented or tells us the frequency of the items. The bars touch with grouped data but with separate items the bars do not touch.

He stops off at a local *bar* to get a drink before heading home. Our bartender used to be a champion weightlifter.

The bar tender pours him a *tall* drink. Disk is overjoyed at how *high* it goes.

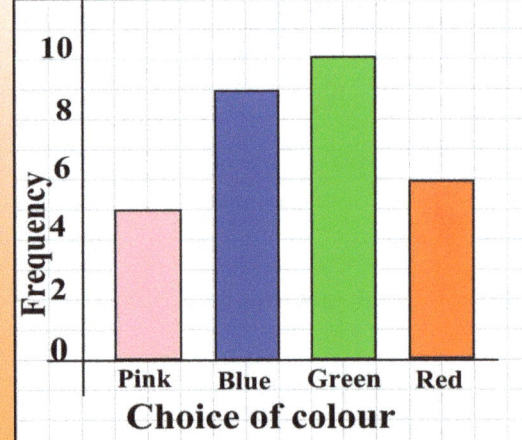
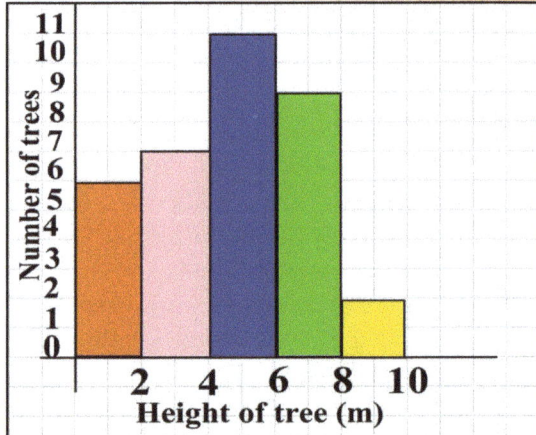

This bar chart compares totally separate items so the *bars are separate*.

All the bars in this chart are for height and you therefore must put every possible height into one bar or the next so there *cannot be any spaces*.

Pie Charts: A pie chart is a circular chart divided into *sectors*. In a pie chart, the *size of the sectors* represents the number of items represented or their frequency. The total of what you want to represent must always *equal to 360^0*. A rebellious angel means 360^0.

Drinking has made him hungry so he drops by at a local *pie shop* to get something to eat.

Just then a *rebellious angel* appears and tries to chop up a pie into rather large *sectors* with his axe!

This pie chart shows how 300 pupils travel to school.

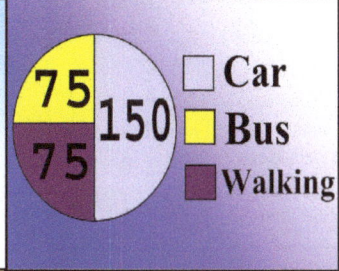

So 360^0 is shared between 300 pupils.
$360^0 \div 300 = 1.2^0$ per pupil.
1.2^0 is called the **Multiplier.**

To draw the pie chat accurately, just multiply 1.2^0 by each total.
This gives the number of degrees for each part:
So $150 \times 1.2^0 = 180^0$
$75 \times 1.2^0 = 90^0$

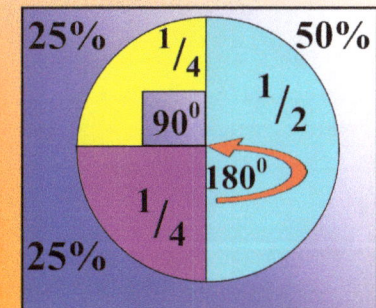

Some angles and fractions that you should know:

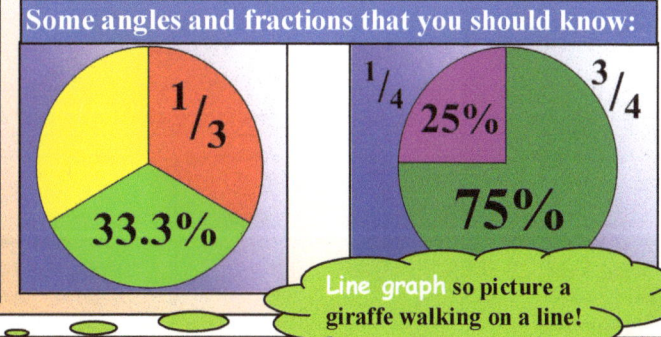

Line graph so picture a giraffe walking on a line!

Line Graphs or Frequency Polygons: Here a *set of points* are joined up by a *straight line*. They show how one set of values change in relation to another.

Disk runs out to get help from a policeman and finds him making a drunken *giraffe* walk the *line*.

As a further test the officer makes giraffe hang some *points on a line!*

This graph might be showing us how the number of books sold changes over the years.

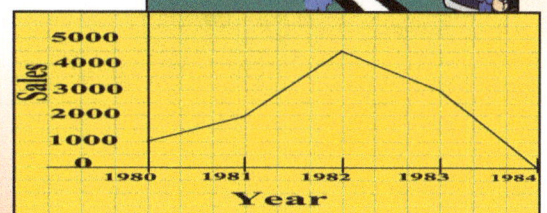

Copyright © Sunnil Singh 2008

Scatter Diagrams: These use *points* set out in different ways. They show the kind of *correlation/relationship* between two things.
Example: the relationship/correlation between ice cream sales and temperature.

As night falls, data leaves the crazy city behind. In the sky stars are *scattered*, some set out in *different ways*.

He stops to take a picture of two stars forming a wonderful *relationship*!

Positive: the values seem to go 'up'. Means that as one variable/item increases so does the other.

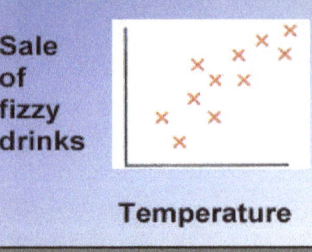

Negative: the values seem to go 'down'. Means that as one variable or item increases the other decreases.

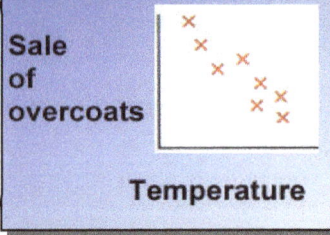

Strong correlation: Means that the points lie closer to each other. There is a good relationship between the variables as they are closely related.
Weak correlation: Means that the points lie further apart. There is a weak relationship between the variables since they are not closely related.

No correlation: Means that there is no relationship between the two variables.

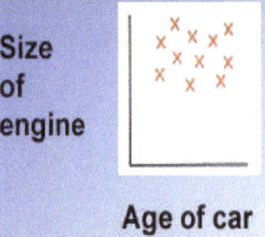

Line of best fit: Passes as close to as many of the values as possible. Usually seems to go through the 'middle' of the data.

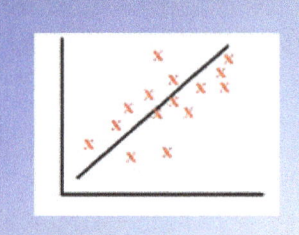

Pictograms: These use *pictures* to represent numbers. Every pictogram will have a *key* to tell you how many items each picture represents.

His camera won't take any *pictures*, so he rushes back to the city to find a camera shop.

The *key*-head assistant has no clue of what to do!

Look at the pictogram showing the number of cups of ice creams sold over 3 days at Mikes Delight.

Number of ice creams sold:
Friday = 35
Saturday = 20
Sunday = 40

All the pictures must be the same size.

Stem and leaf diagrams: Shows *ordered data* in a concise way.

Disk is now furious but is soon arrested for his poor conduct by an officer wearing some *stem and leaves*!

He is then *ordered* to jail along with some other *numbers*.

Example: Arrange the following data in a stem and leaf diagram:
55 48 33 29 18 11 21 30 41 54 47 25 15 47 24 12 47 23 12 42 50 24

```
Stem  | Leaves
  1   |
  2   |
  3   |
  4   |
  5   |
Key: 1 | 2   means 12 items
```

First draw the '**stem**'. The largest number in your data will determine when you stop. Our largest number is 55 so we stop at 5.

```
Stem  | Leaves
  1   |
  2   |
  3   | 33
  4   |       48
  5   | 55
Key: 1 | 2   means 12 items
```

Now fill in the data using the **units' digit** of each number to help you place it in the **correct row**. Strike off the numbers in your data as you proceed.

```
Stem  | Leaves
  1   | 1  2  2  5  8
  2   | 1  3  4  4  5  9
  3   | 0  3
  4   | 1  2  7  7  7  8
  5   | 0  4  5
Key: 1 | 2   means 12 items
```

Fill in all the data and keep them **in order** within each row. From this diagram we can easily see that **11 is the smallest number and 55 the largest.** (Range= 55-11=44)

Mode (most frequent) is 47.

Cool Fact: The best selling copyright book is the Guinness World Records. Over 100 million copies sold worldwide as of June 2001.

You have a go: Arrange these numbers in a stem and leaf diagram: 22, 16, 45, 57, 52, 28, 12, 34, and 38.

Tally/Frequency Tables

Tally means to count, so picture a table counting.

Note: frequency just means 'how many'

|| = 2 and |||| = 5 Tally marks are done using single marks for 1 to 4 and a 'gate' for 5.

Example: Find the frequency of the vowels (a, e, i, o, u) as they appear in the following quotation: 'In mathematics you don't understand things. You just get used to them.'   Von Neumann, Johann (1903 - 1957)

Just highlight or *strike off* the letters *as you count them*.

Immediately *make a tally mark* in the correct column.

'In m**a**th**e**m**a**t**i**cs y**o**u d**o**n't **u**nd**e**rst**a**nd th**i**ngs. Y**o**u j**u**st g**e**t **u**sed t**o** them.'

Letter	Tally	Frequency
a	|||	
e	||||	
i	|||	
o	||||	
u	||||	
	Total	

Bored with his job, he dreams of being a boxer. He *strikes a letter* that is then out for the *count*.

True to his nature he would then *mark* each victory!

Fill in the last column by *adding each tally*.

The *total* should be the same as the total of all the letters you struck off.

Letter	Tally	Frequency
a	|||	3
e	||||	5
i	|||	3
o	||||	4
u	||||	5
	Total	

Letter	Tally	Frequency
a	|||	3
e	||||	5
i	|||	3
o	||||	4
u	||||	5
	Total	20

Addition has to collect each tally.

Tally then *totals* up to see how well he has done!

Cool Fact: The first known census was taken by the Babylonians in 3800 BC, nearly 6000 years ago!

You have a go: Find the frequency of the vowels from the words on this page.

challenge

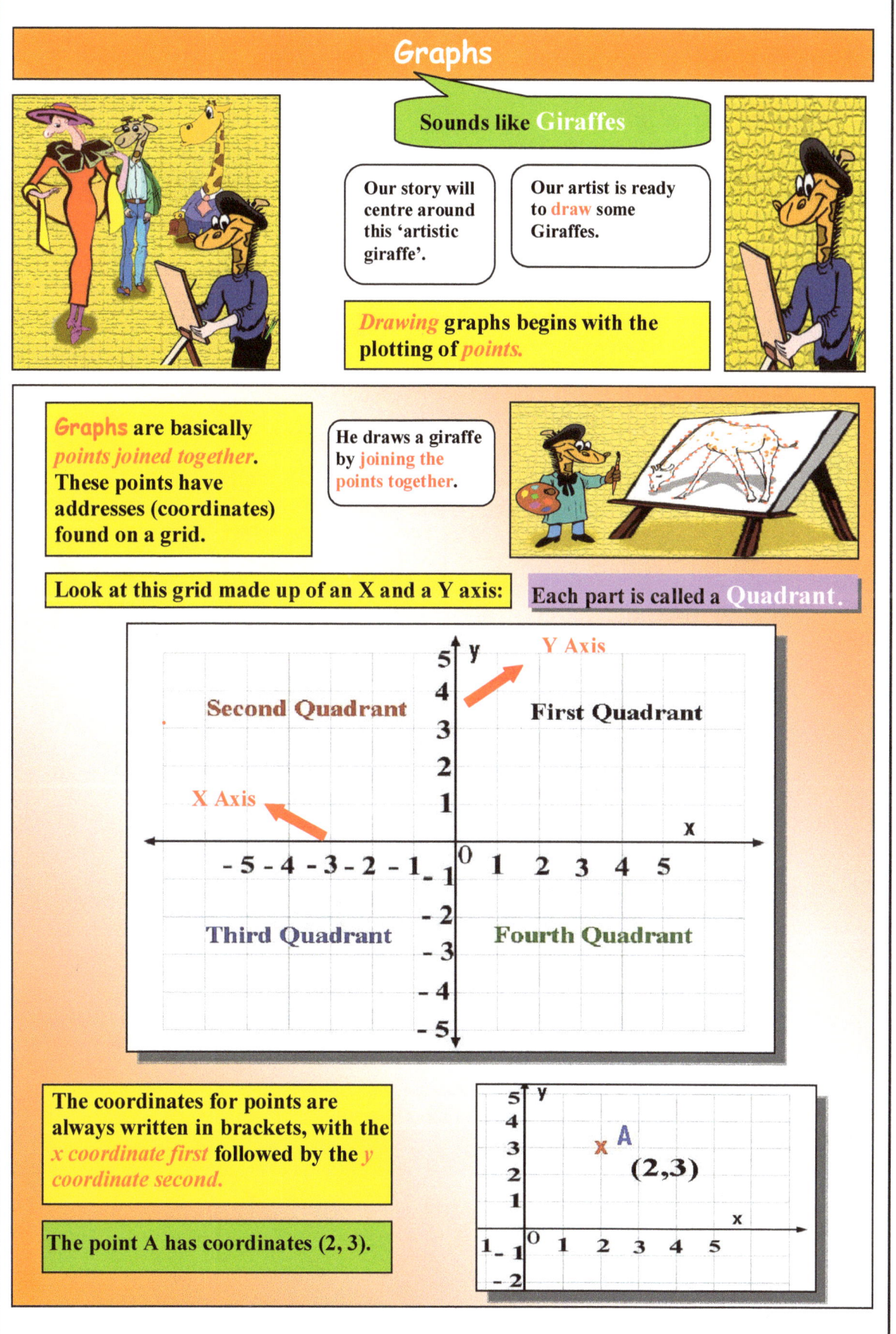

Finding the coordinates of points

When looking to read off points an easy way to remember this is by comparing the reading of points to being the same as walking up some stairs. We *go across* the landing and *then up* the stairs.

However, some of the points escape and he goes looking to *find* his points!

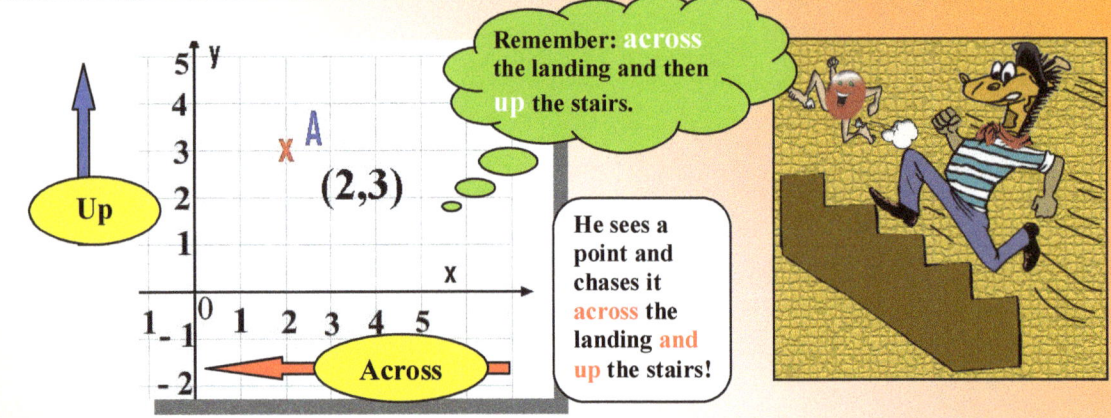

Remember: across the landing and then up the stairs.

He sees a point and chases it across the landing and up the stairs!

The coordinates can have different signs depending on the quadrant they lie within.

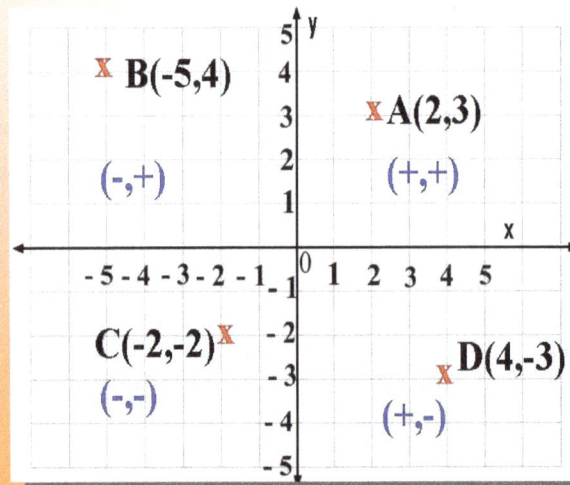

In the First Quadrant both points will be positive.
In the Second Quadrant the X is negative and the Y is positive.
In the Third Quadrant both points will be negative.
In the Fourth Quadrant the X is positive and the Y negative.

Here are some examples of straight line graphs that you should know:

Here every x value is equal to every y value.

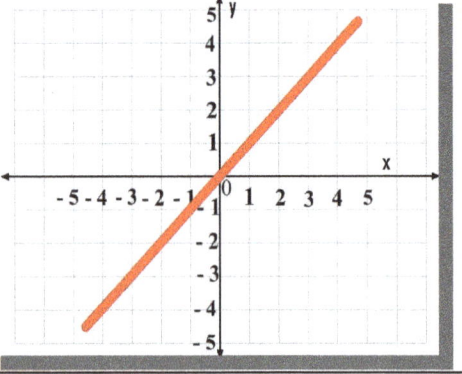

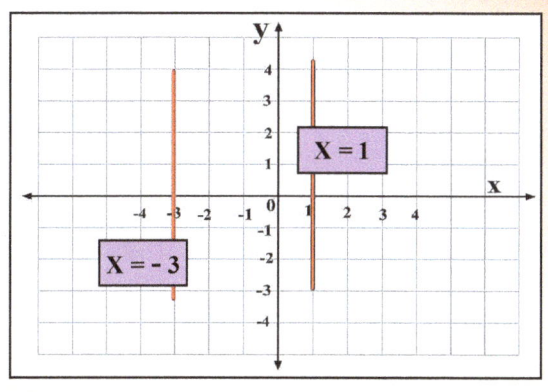

Here the x value stays the same while the y value changes.

Here the y value stays the same while the x value changes.

Drawing graphs from a table.

Picture giraffes on a table.

Example: Draw the graph of $y = 2x + 1$

First: Select some x values, example from -2 to 2. (Take any values but usually some negative and some positive values).

x	-2	-1	0	1	2
y=2x+1					

The giraffes jump of the table so the artist brands a giraffe with a red hot 'X'. How cruel!!!

Second: Substitute into the equation and get the corresponding y values.

x	-2	-1	0	1	2
y=2x+1	-3	-1	1	3	5

Giraffe's friends come to help and shoot the artist with 'Y' shaped slings!

Third: Plot the points and then join them up to get the graph. Easy!

Giraffe also gets his revenge since he now gets to draw the artist!

Cool Fact: Safecracking can be done using graphs! The experienced safecracker listens carefully to the turning dial to determine the number of wheels and contact points inside the lock. He plots this on a graph (on his computer) to find where the points meet. This gives all possible lock combinations.

You have a go:

Draw the graph of:
$y = 3x - 1$.

Mean: This is the total (sum) of all the values ÷ the number of values.

Remember: addition is a shiny dish and division is a deer with good vision.

Picture a mean mother shark.

The *mean* mother shark appears and collects/*adds* all the surfers together onto *a dish*, ready to eat them.

She then gets *division* to light a fire so that she can cook them!

Example: Find the **mean, mode, median** and **range** of the following numbers:
1, 5, 9, 7, 2, 5, 8, 4

First: Arrange them in order: 1 2 4 5 5 7 8 9
This always makes it easier to work with especially for the median.
Then work out the various averages.

Mode: most common value, which is 5.
Median: the middle value:

The numbers must first be in order: 1 2 4 5 5 7 8 9

← 3 numbers on this side   3 numbers on this side →

When there are 2 numbers in the middle the median is halfway between them. You could also strike off one number at a time from each side until you are left with the middle number or numbers.

$$\text{Mean} = \frac{\text{total (sum)}}{\text{Number of values}} = \frac{1+2+4+5+5+7+8+9}{8} = \frac{41}{8}$$
$$= 5.13$$

Range: how far from the largest to the smallest value, i.e. from 9 to 1 = 8

Cool Fact: On average lightening strikes the earth about 100 times every second.

You have a go: Find the **mean, mode, median** and **range** for the following values: 16, 23, 9, 3, 56, 9, 2

Frequency Tables (Grouped Data)

Sometimes it makes more sense to place our data into **groups**.
What if you were a teacher and you wanted to know how many pupils scored between 80-100 for a test? The best way would be to use a Tally/Frequency table with grouped data. Remember the inequality signs from the section on **The Four Mathematical Operators**.

Look at this: $\quad 20 \leq S < 40$

The value of S lies between 20 and 40, but: 20 could be *less than or equal* to S because of the $\leq$ symbol. S will be *less than* 40 but *not equal* to it because of the $<$ symbol.
This all means that the smallest value in this group would be 20 but the largest will only be 39. 40 will have to go into the next group!

Now let's say we wanted to find out how many pupils scored between 80 – 100 in a test
Here are the results:

11   23   58   13   21   34   55   89   14   42   33   37
76   10   98   71   59   72   58   92   35   86   99   93

Remember to strike off each value as it is placed in the table, so that you don't forget any values. This **frequency table** can now be used to draw a **Histogram** (a Bar Chart where the bars touch). Scores are given as a percentage.

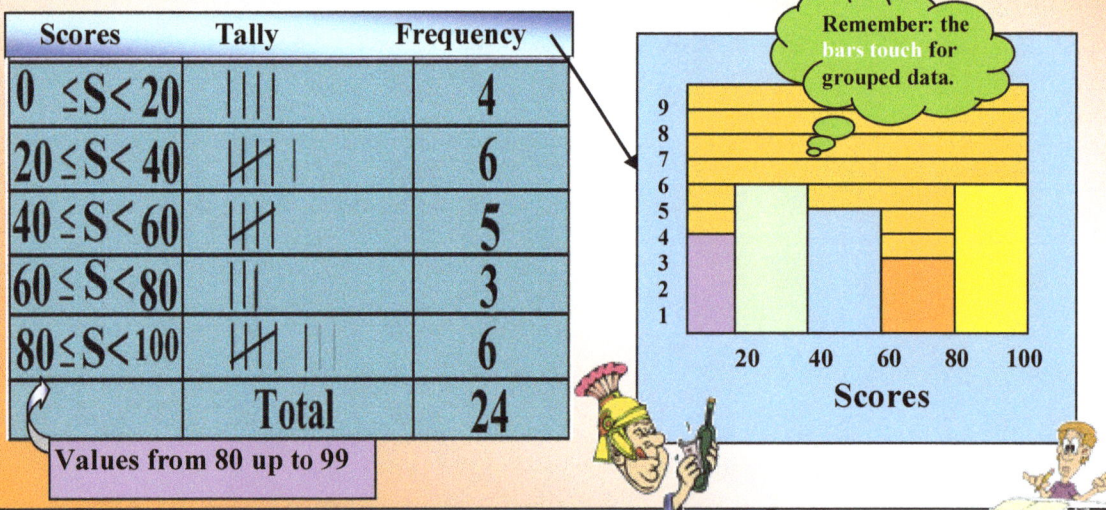

Scores	Tally	Frequency
$0 \leq S < 20$	||||	4
$20 \leq S < 40$	|||| |	6
$40 \leq S < 60$	||||	5
$60 \leq S < 80$	|||	3
$80 \leq S < 100$	|||| |||	6
Total		24

Values from 80 up to 99

Remember: the bars touch for grouped data.

Cool Fact: In ancient times people sent encrypted messages. They substituted one letter for another. Certain letters occur more often in the English language than others. By *counting the frequency* of the letters in a coded message they could match up the letters and so crack the code.

You have a go: In which group would the number 10 lie, A or B?
A) $0 \leq N < 10$
B) $10 \leq N < 20$

Probability

Think of a **game of dice** to help you remember probability.

Probability simply refers to *how likely* something is to happen. We refer to these as *events*.

How likely is either one of these chaps to win?

Lets' see if we can get someone to help!

Probability Scales

There are basically 3 ways to find probabilities:

1) Calculate the probabilities. These are easiest with Equal probabilities and some Unequal probabilities. Example: getting a 4 on a dice is $^1/_6$.

The first person to try and help is a computer geek who tries to *calculate the probabilities* on his computer!

2) Doing a test or a survey. Usually for unequal probabilities. **Example:** to find the probability that a car passing the school will be red, do a survey of the colours of the cars passing the school.

Next we have 2 students. One conducts a *test* while the other carries out a *survey*.

3) Looking back at past data. **Example:** to find the probability that it will rain on a day in June, look at the number of days it rained in June in past years.

Lastly we have a scientist looking at our *data* disk!

Copyright © Sunnil Singh 2008

| Probabilities can only have a value **between 0 and 1.** |

We can use **both numbers and words** on a probability scale as shown:

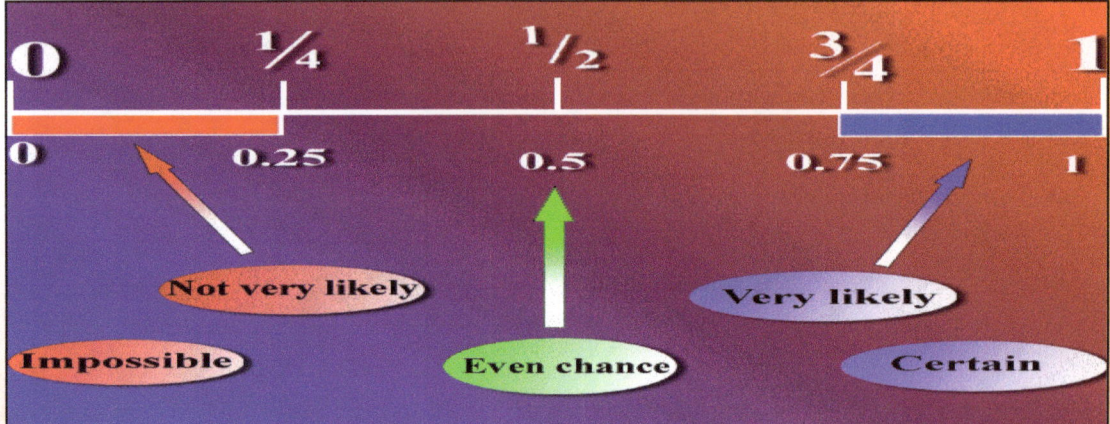

Equal probabilities:
When events have the same chance of happening then we say that they have equal probabilities or that they are equally likely to occur.

These are popular examples:
a) The chance of getting a head or a tail on a coin ($\frac{1}{2}$).
b) The chance of getting any of the numbers on a fair six sided dice ($\frac{1}{6}$).
   The chance of a spinner stopping on a particular colour of equal sections example: 4 colours in equal sections ($\frac{1}{4}$).

Unequal Probabilities:
When events do not have the same chance of happening.

Some common examples:
a) The chance of getting a blue ball from a bag containing 6 blue, 2 red and 10 green balls.

   Answer: $\dfrac{\text{Number of blue balls}}{\text{Total number of balls}} = \dfrac{6}{18}$

There is a simple method to use here. Just work out the probabilities using the following:

$$\dfrac{\text{The number of ways that the event can happen}}{\text{The total number of possible outcomes}}$$

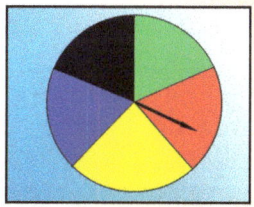

$$P = \frac{\text{Number of red sections}}{\text{Number of sections in total}} = \frac{1}{5}$$

Be careful of many real-life situations where the probabilities are not equal. Some examples: a) The chance of a student winning a race with three contestants (not $\frac{1}{3}$!). One might be more athletic than another.
b) Choosing a bag of crisps from a choice of four different flavours (not $\frac{1}{4}$). You might prefer one type more than the others.

Probabilities always add up to one.

Basically this means that the chance of the opposite happening is simply the rest of the probability that is left over.
Example: What is the chance of there being no snow if the probability of snow is 0.7? Look at the probability scale below:

Probability (no snow) = 1 − 0.7
= 0.3

```
0                                               1
         0.7                    0.3
```

Listing all outcomes.

You will often be asked to list all the possible outcomes *when 2 or more events happen at the same time*. **Example:** List all possible outcomes when a spinner with 4 numbers on it is spun and a coin is flipped.

		Number on spinner		
Coin	1	2	3	4
H	H1	H2	H3	H4
T	T1	T2	T3	T4

List each event with it's possibilities and then fill in the cells. Called a **Sample Space Diagram.**

There are 8 possible outcomes. T2 is shown once. The probability of a tail and a 2 is $\frac{1}{8}$.

The probability of more than 2 events.

Be as logical as possible. The probability from 2 spinners with 3 sides each is shown below:

Spinner 1   Spinner 2

Yellow + 1   Red + 1   Blue + 1
Yellow + 2   Red + 2   Blue + 2
Yellow + 3   Red + 3   Blue + 3

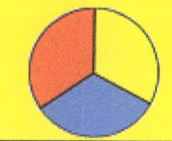 

Cool Fact: What is the probability of toast always seeming to land butter side down when fallen off a table or plate? When it falls, it starts to spin due to gravity but it spins so slowly that it does not have enough time to bring it buttered side up again!

You have a go: What is the probability of getting a red card from an ordinary pack of playing cards?

Recap and Review of Data

1) **Representing data.**
   a) Name some ways of representing data and give a brief explanation of each.
   b) When do we draw bar charts with the bars touching?
   c) The pie chart shows the TV channel that 60 people in a survey most often watched.

   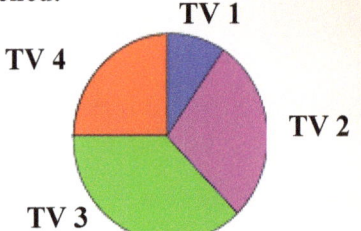

   Which is the most popular channel?
   Which is the least popular channel?
   Which channel is most often watched by 25% of the people in the survey?

   d)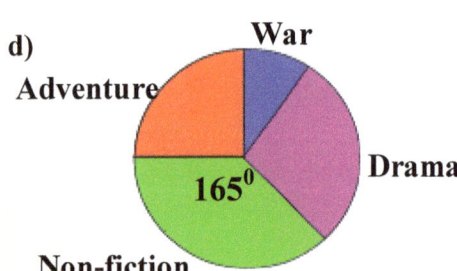

   This pie chart shows the results from all of class A.
   The sector for non-fiction represents 11 pupils.
   How many pupils are in class A?
   Show your working.

   e) Describe the different types of correlation that you have learnt.
   f) What must we always do when drawing pictograms?
   g) On a stem and leaf diagram, what would the key 2 | 6 mean?
   h) How many does the following represent? |||| ||

2) **Graphs**
   a) What are graphs?
   b) Describe how you write the coordinates of a point.
   c) List the 3 basic steps in drawing graphs from a table.

3) **Averages**
   a) Define mode, median, mean and range.
   b) Find these averages for this set of numbers: 6   7   6   5   10   9   46

4) **Frequency tables**
   a) Look at this group: $30 \leq b < 40$. Would you place 30 in this group?

5) **Probability**
   a) Define probability.
   b) List the 3 ways of finding probability.
   c) Distinguish between equal and unequal probabilities.
   d) What is the simple formula that is used to find probability?
   e) Name a diagram used to list all possible outcomes.
   f) List all possible outcomes when a fair 6 sided dice is rolled and a coin is flipped.

   No sweat man!

Your Revision Strategies

My own experience has taught me that information should be taken in (use any strategy or study skills method) and then recalled. Do this several times and this has proven to enhance retention of information.
Listed below are a variety of study skills methods. They can work for any subject.
Feel free to experiment with some of them.

Relevance: Try to find out why you are studying a particular topic. See if you can relate it to things in the world around you. This will make it more interesting for you.

Mnemonics: The introduction of our book describes some mnemonics well suited to mathematics. There are others such as linking the first letter of each keyword to form a silly but memorable rhyme.

Mimes: Make up mimes for key words. The mimes should be something that you can easily picture in your mind and is usually the first thing that you would have thought of when hearing the keyword. The name of the mime must sound like the keyword. We have used this extensively in our book. See how topic headings have mimes associated with them and then linked or developed into a story!

Story: Place all your keywords into a story that links them in a sequence. This is a fun way to remember facts. Again we have used this technique a lot in our book.

Post-its: Write information on post-it notes and place them on a wall, door, large sheet of paper etc. It might be the first thing you see when you get up in the morning.

Ask an expert: Share topics between a few friends in a group and become an expert in a particular area. You better know your stuff!

An imaginary expert: When I was younger I created imaginary friends like Albert Einstein and asked myself how they would solve a particular problem. Often I would pretend to be the expert and force myself to think like them. This helps you overcome any self limitations.

Visualising: As you revise, stop at regular intervals and try to visualise what's going on. With our system just replay the animation or story back in your mind a few times.

Study buddy: Pick someone and arrange to work with them. Try different strategies together like discussion, teaching, reading aloud and questioning each other.

Copyright © Sunnil Singh 2008

Music: Listen to certain music as you revise. Calming music is the best. Try something without words so that your brain will tune in to the lyrics. Try listening to a certain type of music when you revise a certain topic so that the two become linked. Remember that maths and music are very closely related.

Cartoon strips: Draw out your work as a cartoon strip. Include speech and thought bubbles. Use lots of colour and symbols. Try to use stories and characters different from the ones that I have used but are better suited to you individually.

Text messaging: Summarise a topic in only a few spaces. This will make you think about the order and importance. For maths see how well this fits into algebra. If you use a mobile phone you generally abbreviate when you text message.

Mistakes: Find a piece of work with lots of mistakes in them. You then have to find all the mistakes and correct them. Also learn from your own mistakes. If you make a mistake find out what went wrong! This will prevent you from doing it again.

Colour coding: Use different colour paper for different topics. Also underline the words that are linked with each other in the same colour. The colour will be associated with the topic/idea. Try not to use the same colour for similar topics/ideas.
Do you notice how colour has been used in our book?

Alternate solutions: when given a problem try to find as many different ways as possible of getting to the same answer. This works especially well in maths.

Concept mapping: Pick out all the key ideas from a topic. Arrange them on a large sheet of paper. Use arrows to show a flow or a sequence. Write little notes along the arrows. Use similar shapes and colours to connect the same idea or concept.

Teaching: Imagine that you are a teacher. Teach the work that you have to learn as a lesson to some imaginary friends.

Review: Always review your notes/lessons on the same day that you make them. This is especially important in maths as lessons and topics are sequential so learning today's work well will put you in a better position to handle the next topic.

Sit the examination: Take an old examination paper and write it under strict examination conditions. Tell nobody to disturb you. Mark your work with a marking memo from your teacher and then redo the questions that you got wrong. This will help reduce examination nerves as well.

Copyright © Sunnil Singh 2008

Answers
You have a go:

p.10	55 89 144 233 377 610 987 1597
p.11	twenty eight thousand six hundred and fifty seven
p.13	R 273
p.14	a) 1 3 7 21
p.17	a) 0.5 50% b) 0.25 25% c) 0.333 $33\frac{1}{3}\%$ d) 0.75 75%
p.21	6.8 km
p.23	4 places
p.24	a) -84 b) 32
p.26	2.5 1.97 0.987 0.1 0.098
p.28	save £5.25(15% of £35), new cost = £35 - £5.25 =£29.75
p.30	83 89 97
p.33	a) 1: 1.625 b) 1 : 4
p.38	a) 10 b) 100 c) 100 d) 4000
p.39	2
p.41	13:05
p.42	87 841
p.43	Multiplying a one digit number by nine will give a two digit answer where the digits add to nine. Nine subtract five will always give four!
p.48	a) 16.3 1.63 0.163 b) 1 630 16 300 163 000
p.53	angles are: acute, obtuse, right, straight, reflex and revolution.
p.56	$a^0 = 110^0$, $b^0 = 110^0$, $c^0 = 70^0$ and $d^0 = 70^0$
p.57	$a^0 = 100^0$ $b^0 = 40^0$
p.59	a) 4 b) none
p.62	exterior angle = $360^0/6 = 60^0$, interior angle = $180^0 - 60^0 = 120^0$
p.66	$16cm^2$
p.67	$15cm^2/3 = 5cm^2$
p.68	$512cm^3$
p.70	180^0 clockwise
p.73	a) 2 lines b) 3 planes
p.75	scale factor 4
p.77	estimate the number of centimetres and then multiply by 10 to get the number of metres.
p.79	250^0
p.82	a) 14, 16 b) -6, - 10
p.84	3, 7, 11, 15 and 19
p.86	7x7 = 49, 9x9 = 81
p.87	a) 8 b) 9 c) 10
p.88	$18a^2 – 23b + 3b^3$
p.89	a) 8ab – 10ac b) $12x^2 – 24xy$
p.90	answer = 2n + 3
p.91	a) 144 b) 729 c) 10
p.92	$15.5\ ^0C$
p.93	x = 44

p.98

1	2	6
2	2	8
3	4	8
4	5	
5	2	7

p.102

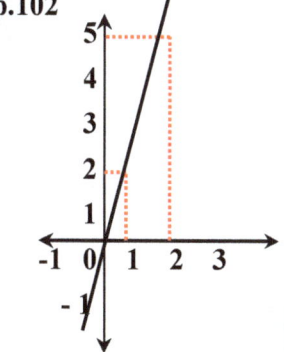

p.104	mode = 9, median = 9, range =54, mean = 16.8
p.105	group B
p.108	P(red) = $^{13}/_{52}$

Answers
Recap and Review

Where the question requires a specific answer not found in the book then the solution is provided. However for most recap questions the page numbers are provided to encourage you to go back and review the entire section.

Section One – Number
1. p. 10
2. p. 11
3. a) p. 14
   b) factors (144) = 1,2,3,4,6,8,9,12…
4. (a-d)-p. 15 to p. 17 e) $7^1/_7$
5. p. 18 , p. 21
6. a) p. 22   b) – 55
7. a) p. 24   b) – 1.618
8. p. 25 , p. 26
9. (a-b)-p. 27 to p. 28   c) £ 30.50
10. (a-c)-p. 29 to p. 30   d) 23,29
11. (a-c)-p. 31 to p. 33   d) 3 shares = £9
    4 shares = £12
12. p. 33
13. p. 34 – p.37
14. p. 39
15. p. 40

Section Two – Shapes
1. p. 50 , p. 51
2. 2.1 360^0 2.2 supplementary angles
   2.3 equal 2.4 equal
3. a) $2x + 80^0 = 180^0$
   $2x = 100^0$
   $x = 50^0$
4. a) g^0 b) h^0
5. 90^0 clockwise
6. 7 sides
7. p. 58
8. p. 65
9. p. 68 , p. 67
10. p. 71 , p. 72
11. p. 74

Section Three – Algebra
1. 1.1 p. 81 , p. 82
   1.2 a) 14 and 16   b) -6 and -10
   1.3 a) add 3   b) divide by 10
2. 2.1 – 2.3 p. 83 , p. 84
   2.4

Pattern number	1	2	3
Number of squares	4	6	8

   n^{th} term = $2n + 2$
3. (3.1-3.4)- p. 85 – p. 87
4. 4.1 a) $2 + 2x$ b) $8y + 5$ c) $3a+10$
   4.2 a) $7xy – 4$ b) $7t + 5y – 2$ c) $3a^2-5b^2-6b$
5. 5.1 make them equal 5.2 $x = 22$
6. $36xy – 72y$
7. a) Paul's number= $2n + 3$
   b) $5n – 8 = 27$
   $5n = 35$
   $n = 7$
8. 8.1 p. 91   8.2 a) 216   b) 6
9. F = 9/5 C + 32
   = 9/5 x 200 + 32
   = 392 ^oF
10. a) b = 3   b) x = 1

Section Four – Data
1. a) p. 95 – p. 98
   b) p. 95 , p. 105
   c) most popular – TV3
      least popular – TV1
      25% watch – TV4
   d) $165^0/11 = 15^0$ therefore 1
      pupil = 15^0, Class A = 360/15 = 24 pupils.
   e) p. 97
   f) p. 98
   g) It would represent the number 26.
   h) A tally of 7
2. a) p. 100
   b) p. 100
   c) p. 102
3. a) p. 103
   b) mode = 6, mean = 89/7 = 12.7
      median = 8, range = 41
4. yes
5. a) to e) from p. 106 – p. 108
   f)

Coin	Dice					
	1	2	3	4	5	6
H	H1	H2	H3	H4	H5	H6
T	T1	T2	T3	T4	T5	T6

Copyright © Sunnil Singh 2008

www.ingramcontent.com/pod-product-compliance
Lightning Source LLC
Chambersburg PA
CBHW061418090426
42743CB00026B/3492